NUMEROLOGY

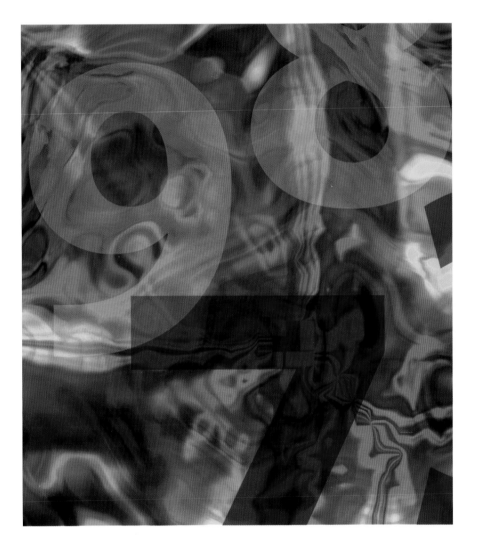

WILLIAM FIELD

Bath · New York · Singapore · Hong Kong · Cologne · Delhi · Melbourne

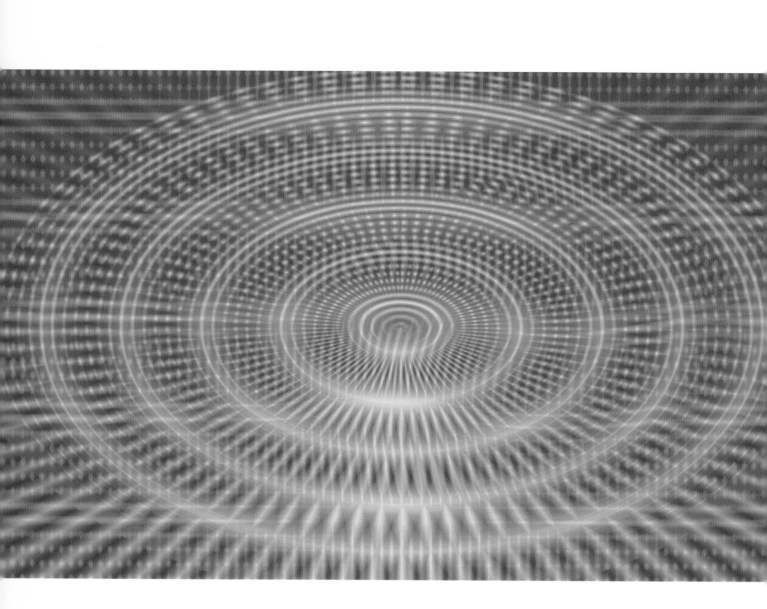

above Numbers and the symbols that represent them are found in every possible facet of the universe, and can be used to describe everything from geometric shapes to the endlessness of infinity.

First published by Parragon in 2009

Parragon Books Ltd
Queen Street House
4 Queen Street
Bath, BA1 1HE

Conceived and produced by **Focus Publishing**, Sevenoaks, Kent
Project editor: Guy Croton
Designer: Philip Clucas
Indexer: Caroline Watson
See page 80 for photograph copyright details

ISBN 978-1-4075-7785-2

Printed in China

CONTENTS

INTRODUCTION TO NUMEROLOGY

Numerology is the term used for the ancient study of numbers and how they relate to our lives. It is a philosophy that draws from many different influences, many of which are several thousand years old. At that early stage in our history, people struggled to understand the world around them, and as a result put a huge amount of effort into quantifying the things they saw and experienced. This interest may well have been engendered by the need to predict the seasons from the movements of the stars.

right Numerology was an important component in the rituals of many primitive civilizations, and was often linked to the movements of the moon.

opposite page, top Stonehenge is one of the oldest man-made structures in the world, and although the experts continue to argue about its original purpose, there is little doubt that some kind of astrology was involved.

Such matters were far more important in those days, as the supply of food was inextricably bound up with nature's cycles. The penalties for making bad decisions were extreme—getting it wrong would result in the young, old, and infirm dying from malnutrition or disease. Consequently, if communities were to thrive, it was vital to have an intimate understanding of the yearly clock. With this knowledge, it became possible to ensure that crops were planted at the right time. In a similar manner, hunters and fishermen had the advantage of knowing when in the year to look for the animals with which they fed their families.

Astrology arose from beliefs centered around early discoveries in astronomy—the cycles of the planets and the positions of the constellations being especially significant. A vitally important component in being able to determine when things like the solstices would occur was, of course, the ability to manipulate numbers. As the result of observing such natural phenomena,

people began to look for patterns in human behavior, and conclusions were drawn from what they saw. Over the years, this developed into a wide variety of complex spiritual philosophies, including such examples as astrology, alchemy, clairvoyance, various forms of mysticism, and numerology. Many early pagan societies were more or less entirely based on them; however, some of the later mainstream religions regarded such activities as occultism. In some cases, certain elements were subsumed into accepted practice. However, others were considered to be the work of the devil, and anyone who followed them risked being labeled as a heretic. In many parts of the world being branded in such a way often resulted in torture and death.

Numerology's primary appeal is that it can help to bring order to things that otherwise appear to be totally chaotic. There are two main

far right The power of numbers was often called upon during occult practices—here King Arthur's half-sister, the sorceress Morgan le Fay, can be seen in the act of casting a spell.

ways in which this is achieved. Firstly, by using those components which are already in numeric form—usually this is the day, month, and year of birth. The second works by converting things which are represented in letter form into numerals. Typically this is part or all of the full birth name.

The three main forms of numerology in use today are Western or "Pythagorean," "Chaldean," and Hebrew or "Kabbalah." Each of these has its adherents, and will have good reasons as to why theirs is superior to the others. This book is based on the Western form, which translates the 26 letters of the alphabet into the numbers 1–9 using a basic chart, as seen here:

There are many different numerological tools, each of which is used to identify or reveal certain personal characteristics. These can include such things as how you are perceived by other people, what your main challenges in life may be, and which aspects of your personality may be holding you back from achieving your full potential. The Soul Urge, for instance, is a concept that is used to reveal what your innermost desires are, as well as the things that you love or hate. These aspects are identified by examining the occurrence of the vowels that are used in your name.

LUCKY CLOVER (4) The four-leaf clover has been considered "lucky" since time immemorial, both for its rarity and the numerological associations of the number four.

1	2	3	4	5	6	7	8	9
A	B	C	D	E	F	G	H	I
J	K	L	M	N	O	P	Q	R
S	T	U	V	W	X	Y	Z	

The Letter-Number conversion chart

Numerology is a fascinating and ancient study of numbers which can reveal much about the world and your life.

THE HISTORY OF NUMBERS

The exact history of the earliest forms of writing is shrouded in the mists of time. Archeologists have discovered a large number of ancient objects marked with rudimentary pictograms across south-eastern Europe. These have been dated to over nine thousand years ago, and belonged to people from a civilization known as the Vinca culture. So many artefacts have been found with these markings on them that they clearly had a definite purpose; however, the exact meaning of these symbols has not been deciphered.

It is not known whether this was the first primitive form of writing. Another contender for this title comes from China, where carved tortoiseshells have been unearthed from 8,600-year-old Neolithic grave sites. These featured character symbols that bear distinct similarities to later Chinese Shang Dynasty writing. Amongst these were what are thought to be representations of the numbers 8 and 20.

Over the next few thousand years writing evolved significantly, with one form being developed by the Sumerians, in a region that now forms part of Iraq. Once again, this was based on a pictogram script. Another, similar symbol system was being used by the Indus civilization in Pakistan at around the same time. It is thought that the drive behind the evolution of writing was economic—as trading developed, people needed to have ever more elegant ways of recording their business activities.

The first Ancient Egyptian writing arose around 5,200 years ago; however, as it was used for both military and financial communications, only certain people were taught how to use it. Although this secrecy persisted for many centuries, other cultures developed their own writing systems on a less elitist basis. Toward the end of the Bronze Age, several alphabets

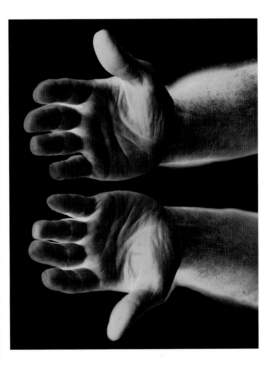

above *One of the main reasons that we use a decimal counting system is that we have ten fingers. If we had twelve, it is probable that a duodecimal (base-12) system would have been adopted instead.*

had appeared, and by the mid-Iron Age, the forerunners of Aramaic and Greek writing had been established. The Latin character set which is still used throughout the Western world came into use in the eighth century BC.

There were many different ways of representing numbers in the ancient world, with the Roman numeral system being one of the best known. This was derived from the Etruscan culture, and used certain letters to represent particular values. Although these have since been replaced for most purposes with the Arabic numerals we use today, they can still be seen in many places. These include such things as book and movie publication dates, clock faces, and architectural structures. The Roman numeral set evolved over time, with the most significant changes being made during the Middle Ages—the form

I	= 1	VI	= 6	L	= 50
II	= 2	VII	= 7	C	= 100
III	= 3	VIII	= 8	D	= 500
IV	= 4	IX	= 9	M	= 1000
V	= 5	X	= 10		

we know today is shown above. For example, 1999 would be written as: MCMXCIX, whereas the year 2000 is simply: MM.

below *Roman numerals are still in common usage to this day, particularly on clock faces and such like. They are perceived as having a touch of class and style about them.*

Bible numerology

There is frequent mention of certain numbers being significant in the Bible. This is not surprising when we take into account the fact that numerology was so important in Judaism, and the huge amount of influence it had on early Christianity. The number 10, for instance, was considered to be particularly special by Pythagoras as well as the Hebrews. It is therefore understandable that there were ten commandments, as these were amongst the most important components in the Bible.

1 As the number 1 represents the Unity, it features regularly—especially in phrases where the Lord God is referred to as "The One." The first of the Ten Commandments "Thou shalt have no other gods before me" reinforced the principle of there being only one God.

2 The number 2 is a common occurrence—there are, for instance, two testaments—the "Old" and the "New." God created two sexes —Man and Woman. There are alternatives, light and dark, good and evil, and so on.

3 The number 3 is also very important—the Holy Trinity of Father, Son, and Holy Ghost, for example. There are also many others—Thought, Word, and Deed, as well as Body, Soul, and Spirit.

4 The number 4 is considered to be the number of creation, as well as the four seasons and the four points of the compass.

7 The number seven has long been associated with perfection and luck—indeed, it is often referred to as God's number. It took God seven days to create the Earth, for instance. When Jesus fed the five thousand, he had two fishes and five loaves, making a total of seven items.

left In Christianity, the God entity symbolized the number 1. This magnificent gilded depiction shows the Lord God seated on a throne and surrounded by adoring angels.

12 The number 12 can be seen in lots of places in the Bible—there were 12 tribes of Israel, 12 Apostles, and 12 angels.

40 The number 40 is seen on numerous occasions in the Bible, and is often considered to represent a period of protracted trial: the Israelites spent 40 years in the wilderness; it rained for 40 days and nights during the Great Flood; Moses twice spent 40 days on the mountain with God; Goliath terrorized the people for 40 days before being killed by David.

Others There are lots of other instances in the Bible where certain numbers are held to have special significance. In the New Testament, for example, is probably the most famous occurrence of a "special number"—666 is referred to as the "Number of the Beast"—elsewhere it is called the "Number of the Antichrist."

left The famous artist Hieronymus Bosch (c.1450–1516) created a host of religious works, with many—such as that seen here—depicting the punishment of sinners.

THE THREE MAIN FORMS

The three most widely recognized forms of numerology are known as the "Chaldean," "Kabbalah" (or "Qabala"), and "Western" (or "Pythagorean") number systems—which historically originated in this order. They differ in very specific ways—for instance, while the Chaldean and Western systems are based on numerical interpretations of a letter's position in the alphabet, the Kabbalah method is derived from a letter's sound. The other main difference is that while the Western and Kabbalah systems use the numbers 1–9, the Chaldean system only uses 1–8, as the number nine is held to have sacred significance.

The Chaldean number system

Although the Chaldean number system has historic links with both Indian Vedic and Kabbalah numerology, it is distinct from them. It is known that it arose in the Persian Gulf region that lies between the Tigris and the Euphrates, in what used to be called Babylonia, but is now part of Iraq. What is not known is exactly when it was first established—it is certainly the oldest of the foremost numerological systems, and is likely to be several thousand years old. Each letter is assigned to a number based on the sound of the letter, and as a result those with similar phonetics are grouped together. The consequent numerical interpretations of a person's name and birthdate can then be used to reveal a variety of important attributes such as personality, soul desires, and challenges.

above *The various numbers have different meanings, depending on where they are used. A Lifepath number of 5, for example, is typically associated with change and restlessness.*

Different systems of numerology use various sequences of numbers at their heart.

The letters of the alphabet are assigned to the numbers 1–8 thus:

1	2	3	4	5	6	7	8
A	B	C	D	E	U	O	F
I	K	G	M	H	V	Z	P
J	R	L	T	N	W		
Q		S		X			
Y							

NUMBER 9 The number 9 is not used in Chaldean numerology, as it is considered to have sacred significance. There are no such restrictions in Western numerology, however, where it is usually associated with humanitarian attributes.

Kabbalah or Qabala numerology

Kabbalah or Qabala numerology arose out of Jewish mysticism—its roots were established around two thousand years ago, when it was believed that the Torah, the first books of the Hebrew Bible, contained hidden meanings. The belief was that these could be interpreted by using Kabbalah numerology, and through this the true meanings of holy teachings, including the Judaic Bible, could be understood. It was originally structured around the Hebrew alphabet, which only has 22 letters. Since those early times, it has been modified twice —firstly for the Greek alphabet (which has 24 letters), and then later to account for the rise to prominence of the 26-letter Roman alphabet.

Unlike the Chaldean and Western systems, the Kabbalah method uses only the letters of the name, and is not combined with the birthdate. This process, which is often referred to as "Gematria," relates the alphabetic letters or syllable sounds to number equivalents. There are, however, many different conventions in use, some of which go well beyond birthdates and names, and are applied to all written words. In this system, the letters that make up a word are converted to numeric values, and these are summed together to generate a key-code for that word. Other words that use the same key-code can then be substituted for it to reveal hidden meanings.

below *The Kabbalah method of numerology evolved in the MIddle East, in what is now the country of Israel.*

Jewish mysticism is the basis of Kabbalah or Qabala numerology.

Western or Pythagorean numerology

It is believed that Western or Pythagorean numerology was established by the charismatic Greek philosopher and mathematician Pythagoras. He was born on the Greek island of Samos in the sixth century BC, and spent much of his adult life in the Greek city-state of Croton in southern Italy. He thought that the entire universe could be expressed numerically, and is widely credited with saying that "The world is built upon the power of numbers." It may well be, however, that he used earlier numerological methods as the basis for his system. His mystic beliefs were strongly influenced by his teachers, who included both Judaic and Indian spiritualists, and he knew the Chaldean system

above The Ancient Greeks had many different belief systems, most of which were based on superstitions of one kind or another.

well. Eventually he opened his own school, where he taught a blend of mathematics, astronomy, and philosophy, as well as mysticism, a major component of which was the connection between life and numbers. The Western system works by sequentially assigning the letters of the alphabet to the numbers 1–9, as shown here:

1	2	3	4	5	6	7	8	9
A	B	C	D	E	F	G	H	I
J	K	L	M	N	O	P	Q	R
S	T	U	V	W	X	Y	Z	

PYTHAGORAS The charismatic Greek philosopher and mathematician Pythagoras based his entire life and philosophy on the study of numbers.

OTHER FORMS OF NUMEROLOGY

Ancient Chinese

The Chinese "Book of Changes" is an ancient text that is also known variously as the "I Ching," the "Yì Jìng," or the "Classic of Changes." It details a series of cosmological and philosophical beliefs that deal with the issue of the inevitability of change. Its foundations probably arose around five thousand years ago, but the I Ching was certainly well established during the Zhou Dynasty (1122 BCE–256 BCE). There is much debate as to who was involved in its compilation—many believe that Confucius was responsible for many of the later parts. The book itself is based on a symbol system that is used in a manner akin to numerology to understand various natural and personal events. These pictograms were mainly used for predictive purposes, and although some practitioners performed divination for good purposes, others subverted them for use in evil ways.

below The Ancient Chinese used a symbol system that was similar to numerology to understand various natural and personal events. Decisions in battle were sometimes based on the assumptions of practitioners in the art of divination.

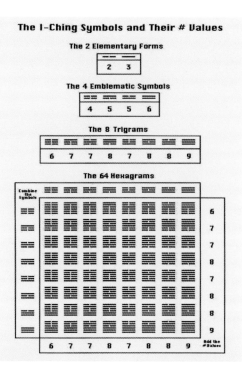

CHINESE BUDDHISM
Chinese Buddhism has many connections with numbers—the Seven Steps of Buddha, which symbolize the ascent of the seven cosmic stages, being a good example.

Ancient Egyptian

The Ancient Egyptians believed that certain numbers had spiritual significance, especially 2, 3, 4, and 7, as well as any other number of which they were prime factors. These concepts were included in a funerary text which these days is usually referred to as the "Book of the Dead." The Ancient Egyptians themselves called it "The spell for coming forth by day." It was typically written on a papyrus, linen, or animal skin scroll, which was placed either close by or in a dead person's coffin. Its purpose was to give the deceased instructions on how to ascend to the afterlife, and once there, how to deal with any problems they may face so that they could be reborn. It was believed that this journey was accomplished in a single night, and that the rebirth would occur the following morning. Thus it was vitally important that the spirit had all the necessary information it could need to achieve this. The main body of the book was therefore composed of around two hundred "helpful" spells.

The Ancient Egyptians used the decimal system *(below)*, with the following hieroglyphs to represent the powers of ten:

EGYPTIAN HIEROGLYPHS Many Ancient Egyptian hieroglyphs used recognizable symbols—the pictogram which represented the letter "L," for example, is in the form of a lion. Pictured above is the mythological Sphinx, a creature which had the body of a lion, and the head of a man.

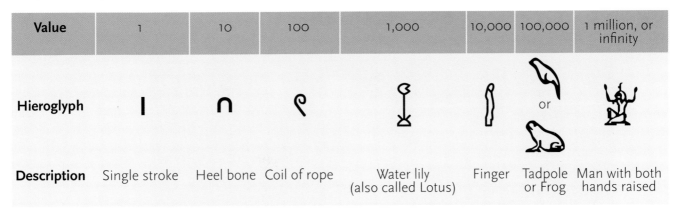

Value	1	10	100	1,000	10,000	100,000	1 million, or infinity
Hieroglyph	I	∩	၆	♉	ℓ	or	🧍
Description	Single stroke	Heel bone	Coil of rope	Water lily (also called Lotus)	Finger	Tadpole or Frog	Man with both hands raised

The Ancient Egyptians accorded special significance to certain numbers and devised various systems.

Northern European

A form of numerology was also practiced long ago in northern Europe—Germanic and Norse pagans believed that the numbers 3 and 9, as well as their multiples, had special powers. This can be seen throughout the mythology from these cultures, with most of the key features being represented in sets of three. Until the Latin character set was adopted, these civilizations wrote with runic alphabets. The Scandinavian variant was named "Futhark," after the sounds of the first six letters. Over time, this alphabet evolved—the version seen below is an early variant from around AD 200. It has 24 letters (as did the Greek alphabet of the same era), made up of 18 consonants and six vowels.

OGHAM STONES Ogham stones are ancient structures that have inscriptions carved into them, and many feature symbols that represent numbers. The little-known writing system is sometimes referred to as the "Celtic Tree Alphabet."

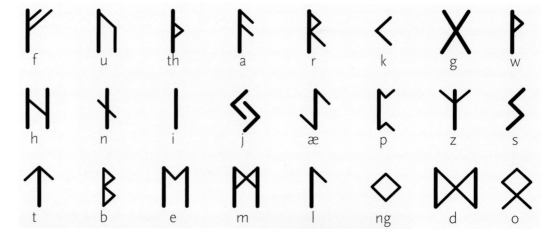

f	u	th	a	r	k	g	w
h	n	i	j	æ	p	z	s
t	b	e	m	l	ng	d	o

right *Pagans wrote with runic alphabets. The Scandinavian variant shown here was known as the "Futhark."*

left *A form of numerology was practiced by early European pagans. This played an important part in many of their rituals—especially in important ceremonies such as funerals, where the body of a recently-fallen warrior was often burned in a flaming ship.*

Mayan

Numerology was not restricted to the Old World —the Mayans were extremely accomplished mathematicians, and had strong religious views on the relationships between numbers and nature. Their civilization, which lasted from around AD 250 to AD 900, grew up in an area that ranged from central Mexico to northern Central America, including present day Belize, El Salvador, Guatemala, and Honduras. They were particularly adept at making astronomical observations, and used these to regulate their calendar. Although we are used to the decimal or "base 10" number system, which is structured around the numbers 0–9, the Mayans used what is known as a vigesimal or "base 20" system. This uses the numbers 0–19, as shown here:

above *The Mayans used their powerful understanding of mathematics in the construction of their distinctive temples.*

Decimal or base 10 system:

| 1 | 10 | 100 | 1000 | 10,000 | 100,000 | 1,000,000 and so on... |

Vigesimal or base 20 system:

| 1 | 20 | 400 | 8000 | 160,000 | 3,200,000 | 64,000,000 and so on... |

0	1	2	3	4
5	6	7	8	9
10	11	12	13	14
15	16	17	18	19

THE KEY COMPONENTS

There are many different components that together form what we know as numerology. These include such things as the Destiny Number, Life Path Number, Personal Year Number, and so on. Each of these is found using specific methods, and the results are interpreted according to basic tenets, based on the attributes of the numbers involved.

NUMBER 6 The number 6 is often associated with romance and matters to do with the family and domesticity.

left Many aspects of numerology were derived from observations made from nature, in which numbers can be represented in many different forms, such as the geometry of the webs constructed by the orb spider.

right The number six is found in many naturally occurring places, such as the number of legs on an insect, or, as pictured here, the number of petals on a flower.

THE DESTINY NUMBER

far right In most instances, multiple-digit numbers are reduced to a single term called an integer. The number 27, for example, would usually be added together to make a 9.

The Destiny or Expression Number is used to reveal what opportunities may come along during a person's lifetime, and how they relate to others around them. In this context, it is important to realize, however, that there is a world of difference between having an opportunity and making something of it.

Find your Destiny Number

Your Destiny Number can be found by taking each part of your name and converting it from letters into numbers. The names you use should be your full birth name as it appears on your birth certificate, and not anything that has been acquired later, such as a nickname, a married name, or an assumed name. These days it is considered valid, however, to use an adopted name if it was given shortly after birth. The resulting numbers are then individually summed to a single digit, and once again added together and reduced to an integer (single number).

below A Destiny Number of 9 is linked with compassion, understanding, and an ability to inspire others.

The letters should be converted using this chart:

1	2	3	4	5	6	7	8	9
A	B	C	D	E	F	G	H	I
J	K	L	M	N	O	P	Q	R
S	T	U	V	W	X	Y	Z	

For example:

My name, William John Field, works out thus:

William = 5 + 9 + 3 + 3 + 9 + 1 + 4 = **34**; 3 + 4 = **7**
John = 1 + 6 + 8 + 5 = **20**; 2 + 0 = **2**
Field = 6 + 9 + 5 + 3 + 4 = **27**; 2 + 7 = **9**
Total = 7 + 2 + 9 = **18**; 1 + 8 = **9**

In this case, my Destiny Number is revealed as **9**—there are two sides to this. The positive aspects of this number are linked with compassion, understanding, and an ability to inspire others. It also indicates creativity, and can lead to a variety of vocations including the arts and careers in such professions as law or medicine. Although such people hold friends and close relationships especially dear, if the negative side is allowed to prevail, the results can lead to self-obsession, an unwillingness to take on board the feelings of others, and a remote personality.

Key features of the Destiny Number

1 The positive aspects of having a 1 Destiny Number are that the combination of your "make it happen" attitude and your inherent ambition will allow you to make the most of any opportunities that come your way. Your independence, determination, and self-confidence mark you out as a natural leader. If the negative aspects are allowed to flourish, then there is the possibility of a fear of routine, as well as the risk of egotism, aggression, and of becoming self-centered.

above *People with a Destiny Number of 5 like to bask in the limelight, but in negative cases can become impatient.*

2 The positive aspects of the 2 Destiny Number are that you will have a natural inclination toward understanding people. This intuition may well manifest itself in some form of peacemaking, and could well lead to spiritual or diplomatic work. Where the negative aspects make themselves known, the individual concerned is likely to be withdrawn—they may well display apathy, anxiety, a loss of confidence, and could also be moody and very sensitive to any form of criticism.

3 The positive aspects of the 3 Destiny Number include a natural optimism, inborn creativity, and the ability to get on well with people. These attributes often lead to opportunities in the arts, the media, or some kind of sales work. If the negative aspects show themselves, it is usually in the form of a shallow character.

4 The positive aspects of the 4 Destiny Number tend to manifest themselves through a well organized manner, with professionalism, creativity, and high standards all to the fore. Sometimes, however, the negative aspects manage to take over the personality, in which case there is a distinct tendency toward becoming narrow-minded and overly pushy. In some circumstances, this can lead to bullying.

5 The positive aspects of the 5 Destiny Number are generally expressed through an ability to comprehend and successfully take on a wide variety of different tasks. These people often also like to bask in the limelight. When taken to extremes, however, the negative aspects can become dominant, and the result is often impatience and restlessness.

6 The positive aspects of the 6 Destiny Number usually give rise to level-headed individuals with a humanitarian approach to life and a loving attitude to those around them. They tend to feel a great deal of responsibility; however, if this goes too far and becomes a negative aspect, then they may well become entrenched and feel justified in interfering in the affairs of those they work or live with.

7 The positive aspects of the 7 Destiny Number may well lead to deep spirituality, with an inherent sense of logic and the desire to strive for perfection. If this takes over, however, the negative aspects of intolerance, and introversion can lead to a lack of outward emotions.

8 The positive aspects of the 8 Destiny Number can generate a well-organized mind that has a great deal of drive. This creates a natural reliability that may well lead to opportunities in senior management. When overdone, however, the negative aspects of stubbornness, dogmatism, and impatience may well come to the fore.

9 The positive aspects of the 9 Destiny Number include such attributes as a love of people, an inherent creativity, and an ability to communicate well. This may well lead to work in the arts or the media, but if the negative aspects are allowed to dominate, then the individual concerned may become thick-skinned to those around them.

THE LIFE PATH NUMBER

The Life Path Number

far right The Life Path Number is found by adding together the individual numbers that make up the birth date. The resulting number is then reduced to a single digit—26, for example, would become "8."

Your journey through life is conducted according to a series of personal characteristics —those you were born with are identified by your Birth Day Number. These then change as you pass through life—your skills, idiosyncrasies, strengths, and weaknesses will develop according to the lessons you learn. It is no surprise therefore, that these have a direct

above The Life Path Number highlights the personal attributes that can have a marked influence on an individual's choice of career.

bearing on the way you behave when faced with the challenges and manifold circumstances that everyone goes through in life. Consequently, when these attributes are interwoven with the advances gained through experience, they have an enormous influence on where life's rich tapestry takes you. This is all represented by what is known as the Life Path Number, a figure which is derived from the sum of the digits in your date of birth.

Find your Life Path Number

The number itself is established by adding together the components that make up your birthdate—note that no abbreviations should be used. My birth year, for example is 1960, not "60." The resultant figure is then reduced to a single digit.

NUMBER 4 The positive aspects of the 4 are linked with practicality, organizational abilities, and dedication.

NUMBER 8 The negative aspects of the 8 can cause the individual concerned to become obsessed with work, resulting in isolation.

For example:

My Life Path Number can be found thus,

My Date of Birth is June 13th, 1960 (06–13–1960); this sums up as below:

$$0 + 6 + 1 + 3 + 1 + 9 + 6 + 0 = \mathbf{26}$$

The first stage therefore gives the number 26, but this is then further reduced to 2 + 6, which leaves the figure **8** as my Life Path Number.

Keywords for the Life Path Numbers

1 With a Life Path Number of 1, the positive aspects are typically related to a personal journey that involves drive, self-reliance, and a belief in one's own abilities. At the same time, it is often associated with a gregarious nature. On the negative side, the number 1 can lead to an inward focus that can result in very selfish behavior and an inability to consider the needs of others.

2 The positive aspects of a Life Path Number of 2 include the likelihood of becoming involved with some form of employment where inherent communication skills can be put to good use. Although the number is linked to idealism, this can be expressed in a negative manner through extremist views, in which case the individual's whole outlook may become self-destructive.

3 The Life Path Number 3 is linked to creativity, enjoying the company of other people, and good communication skills. As such, this can often lead to a career that involves dealing with the public, such as in the media. Should the individual concerned allow the negative aspects of the 3 to take over, then they will be prone to bouts of being oversensitive, sullen, and intolerant.

4 When the positive aspects of the Life Path Number 4 are expressed, the individual is likely to use their practicality, organizational abilities, and dedication to become involved in some kind of senior management or administration role. Should the negative aspects of the number be allowed to dominate, then the person may well become obsessive and entrenched. This will significantly alter both the path and destination of their life's journey.

5 A Life Path Number of 5 signifies a blend of idealism, curiosity, and humanity that together with good communication skills can give rise to great versatility. As such, a person with the positive aspects of this number will find that there are few boundaries on their life's journey. Should the negative aspects be expressed, however, the individual will lose all sense of direction, and may become overly self-indulgent.

6 Where the positive aspects of the Life Path Number 6 flourish, a person with this number will often demonstrate a strong humanitarian streak, together with a high level of domestic responsibility. Where the negative aspects of this number are allowed to show themselves, the person concerned is likely to become over-burdening, critical, and may try to take control of everything around them.

7 The positive aspects of the Life Path Number include a natural intellectual ability as well as a thorough manner. This is often linked with an affectionate and spiritual outlook, and so may well result in a life journey that involves a professional career. On the other hand, should the negative aspects flourish, the individual concerned may become antisocial, introverted, and entrenched.

8 The positive aspects of the Life Path Number 8 usually show themselves through such attributes as self-reliance, organizational abilities, and leadership qualities. As such, the life journey may well include time spent in senior management; however, if the line is crossed the negative aspects will come to the fore. If this happens, the individual concerned may become obsessed with work, which can result in isolation and loneliness.

9 Where an individual has a Life Path Number of 9 that is expressed in a positive manner, their personality is generally associated with a deep and lifelong concern for humanitarian issues. This attribute usually makes them popular with other people, and so their life path typically involves the arts and the media. If the negative aspects take over, then the individual is likely to become oversensitive, critical of others, and often deeply self-centered.

THE BIRTH DAY NUMBER

The Birth Day Number should be used in conjunction with the Life Path Number. The former reveals what attributes and abilities you were born with, while the latter identifies what you can make of them, should you wish to make the effort and learn the lessons. While the Life Path Number is found by adding all the digits of your birth date together, the Birth Day Number is simply the date on which you were born, and is not reduced to a single digit. Consequently, there are 31 different numbers, each of which denotes a specific set of positive and negative attributes. The 31 numbers are examined in detail below.

above *The Birth Day Number should be used in conjunction with the Life Path Number and can reveal what attributes and abilities you were born with.*

Keywords for the Birth Day Number

1 **Positive:** Executive ability. Leadership. Will power. Self-confidence. Sensitive.
Negative: Poor focus. Repressed.

2 **Positive:** Emotion. Sensitivity. Intuition. Sociable. Warm-hearted. Emotional.
Negative: Nervous. Depressive. Moody. Anxious.

3 **Positive:** Vitality. Energetic. Restless. Easygoing. Communicative. Imaginative. Affectionate.
Negative: Poor focus. Superficial. Oversensitive. Moody.

4 **Positive:** Organizer. Responsible. Disciplined. Sincere. Honest. Serious. Hard-working. Rational.
Negative: Repressed. Introverted. Stubbornness. Dogmatic.

5 **Positive:** Sociable. Talented. Versatile. Communicative. Progressive. Imaginative. Adaptable.
Negative: Restless. Impatient. Easily bored. Shirks responsibility.

6 **Positive:** Responsible. Caring. Helpful. Understanding. Open. Honest.
Negative: No negatives.

7 **Positive:** Perfectionist. Individualistic. Analytical. Spiritual. Sensitive. Self-reliant.
Negative: Doesn't take orders well. Self-centered.

8 **Positive:** Organizer. Businessman. Reliable. Honest. Idealistic. Supportive.
Negative: No negatives.

9 **Positive:** Idealistic. Humanitarian. Tolerant. Generous. Sensitive. Sympathetic. Compassionate.
Negative: No negatives.

10 **Positive:** Independent. Leadership. Will power. Self-confidence. Innovative. Sensitive.
Negative: Poor focus. Repressed. Dominating.

11 **Positive:** Idealist. Sociable. Persuasive. Spiritual. Intuitive. Aware. Sensitive. Analytical.
Negative: Temperamental. Dreamer.

12 **Positive:** Vitality. Robust. Communicative. Energetic. Artistic. Imaginative. Rational. Affectionate.
Negative: Restless. Superficial. Poor focus. Moody. Oversensitive.

13 Positive: Organizer. Disciplined. Sincere. Honest. Hard-working. Practical. Rational.
Negative: Dominating. Repressed. Intolerant. Over-perfectionist.

14 Positive: Sociable. Talented. Versatile. Organizer. Communicative. Imaginative. Adaptable.
Negative: Restless. Impatient. Easily bored.

15 Positive: Home-loving. Domestic. Parental. Responsible. Capable. Peaceful. Artistic. Generous.
Negative: Stubborn.

16 Positive: Self-reliant. Home-loving. Spiritual. Technical. Original. Intuitive. Logical. Responsible.
Negative: Loneliness. Inflexible. Introspective. Stubborn.

17 Positive: Honest. Ethical. Shrewd. Successful. Organizer. Ambitious. Goal-oriented.
Negative: Poor focus. Repressed.

18 Positive: Sociable. Individual. Humanitarian. Compassionate. Organizer. Broad-minded.
Negative: Repressed. Dramatic.

19 Positive: Independent. Leadership. Will-power. Self-confidence. Original. Sensitive.
Negative: Self-centered. Poor focus. Repressed. Dominating. Defensive. Loner. Nervous. Angry.

20 Positive: Sensitive. Intuitive. Sociable. Warm-hearted. Affectionate.
Negative: Emotional. Nervous. Depressive. Moody.

21 Positive: Robust. Relaxed. Communicative. Imaginative. Rational. Affectionate. Sensitive.
Negative: Restless. Poor focus. Superficial. Moody.

22 Positive: Original. Organizer. Reliable. Determined. Idealistic. Humanitarian. Charismatic.
Negative: Poor focus. Rigidity. Stubbornness. Repressed. Nervous tension.

23 Positive: Sociable. Talented. Versatile. Communicative. Imaginative. Adaptable. Analytical.
Negative: Restless. Impatient. Easily bored. Shirk responsibility.

24 Positive: Responsible. Compassionate. Peacemaker. Home-loving. Sensitive. Affectionate.
Negative: No negatives.

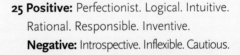

25 Positive: Perfectionist. Logical. Intuitive. Rational. Responsible. Inventive.
Negative: Introspective. Inflexible. Cautious.

26 Positive: Organizer. Sociable. Efficient. Ambitious. Energetic. Co-operative. Adaptable. **Negative:** No negatives.

27 Positive: Selfless. Humanitarian. Self-reliant. Broadminded. Generous. Co-operative. Sensitive.
Negative: No negatives.

28 Positive: Independent. Leadership. Will-power. Self-confident. Original. **Negative:** Repressed.

29 Positive: Idealistic. Imaginative. Creative. Sensitive. Intuitive. Analytical. Sociable. **Negative:** Nervous.

30 Positive: Individuality. Communicative. Dramatic. Imaginative. Artistic. Creative. **Negative:** Opinionated.

31 Positive: Organizer. Energetic. Dependable. Serious. Sincere. Patient. Original. Imaginative.
Negative: Rigid. Stubborn. Repressed. Poor focus.

The Personal Year Number

THE PERSONAL YEAR NUMBER

Everyone has experienced good years and bad years in their lives. In numerology, these are referred to as Personal Years, and they run in nine-year cycles. It is possible to reveal where you are with regard to the universe's annual ebb and flow from your birth date. The events that occur around you—be they your own, or those on a grander scale, are all involved. The Personal Year Number, which is linked to such things as emotional state and energy levels, can be used to deduce how the coming year is likely to turn out for you.

Personal Years can be either good or bad—and everybody experiences both kinds.

Find your Personal Year Number

Finding your personal year number is very straightforward—the number of your birth month is added to your birth day. The resultant number is then added to the year number.

For example

My date of birth is June 13th, 1960, so the month (6) is added to the day (13), to give 19. The 1 and the 9 are then added together, giving 10, and this is, in turn, reduced to 1, since 1 + 0 = **1**.

The year—2009—is also reduced to a single digit = 2 + 0 + 0 + 9 = **11**; 1 + 1 = **2**

This is then added to the 1 derived from the date of birth, resulting in a Personal Year Number of **3**.

Number 30 When a two-digit number that ends in a zero is reduced to an integer, the zero is simply ignored, and so a 30 becomes a 3.

left *Birth is closely associated with astrology, and so is affected by the numerology of the movements of the heavens.*

Keywords for the Personal Year Number

1 The number 1 signifies the start of a new phase in your life—one in which you will have new challenges to face. Before you can take them on, however, you will have to decide what it is that you actually want to achieve. Although the goals you choose in life may not be easily reached, you will have the strength to attain them.

2 The number 2 denotes a year in which you will need to step out of the limelight and bide your time until a more auspicious period comes along. It is a year in which you will have to develop relationships with those around you. The key is to maintain your equilibrium, as you will encounter many stumbling blocks, and patience will be rewarded.

3 The number 3 indicates a year in which relationships —both close personal and wider social ones—will be prominent features. It is a time to savor life and develop your artistic side; however, it is also important to remain focused on your goals, or they will slip away from you while you are out enjoying yourself.

4 The number 4 signifies a year in which it is important to get yourself thoroughly organized. Hard work is the underlying theme in a year like this; however, it is also important that you take the trouble to look after yourself properly, or you will succumb to illness. Good balance is the key.

5 The number 5 signifies a year of new experiences and relationships—a time to break free from the ruts that have been constraining your life. In doing so you will feel that the shackles have dropped away. However, it is important to keep an eye on your goals, or your previous hard work will have been wasted.

6 The number 6 year is a good one as far as your close family and friends are concerned, as positive emotional considerations feature heavily in such a period. As a result, many of the other aspects of your life may have to take a back seat, so this is not a time to expect major achievements to come to fruition. Bide your time and enjoy improved relationships.

7 The number 7 is a year in which you need to concentrate on your own situation and develop your future goals. It is a time of contemplation of past events and for thinking about exactly where you would like to go with your life in the future. It is a good time to improve your talents, especially those which are of an artistic or literary nature.

8 The number 8 denotes a year of personal inner strength, and from this you will have the potential for many significant achievements. In order for them to come to fruition, however, you will need to recognize the opportunities when they appear, and then act on them in a positive manner.

9 The number 9 signifies a year of completion— especially that of long-term projects. It is a good time to take stock of your life, and it may well prove to be appropriate that you devote some of your energies to helping other people in the run-up to the start of another nine-year cycle.

left *The number 3 indicates a year in which relationships —both close personal and wider social ones —will be prominent features. However, the chance to achieve goals must not be ignored.*

The Planes of Expression

THE PLANES OF EXPRESSION

The Planes of Expression were first written about in ancient texts. These detailed the energies of each of the letters in the alphabet, and the way that these are used to make up your birth name has great relevance in numerology. In essence, the set of letters reveals much about the way you behave and what your overall life potential is. It is still up to you to make something of this, however!

The Four Planes of Expression

There are four different planes—they are the Mental (Mind), Physical (Body), Emotional (Soul), and Intuitive (Spirit), and each is linked to specific letters, as can be seen below.

The Mental Plane

The letters that make up the mental plane are A, G, H, J, L, N, and P; they are closely linked with analytical and intellectual skills, especially those involving learning and problem solving.

The Physical Plane

The letters that make up the physical plane are D, E, M, and W; they are associated with things that involve energy and action, such as strength or responses to the five senses (touch, taste, sight, sound, and smell).

The Emotional Plane

The letters that make up the emotional plane are B, I, O, R, S, T, X, and Z; they signify such attributes as innovation, imagination, and sentimentality. They are most obvious to others when you are expressing your feelings.

The Intuitive Plane

The letters that make up the intuitive plane are C, F, K, Q, U, V, and Y; as the name suggests, they are connected with intuition and spirituality. These are essentially personal matters, and may be things you keep to yourself.

right *The Planes of Expression can be used to determine what your primary attributes are—these can have a significant effect on the way you lead your life, and what you are likely to end up doing.*

far right *Some people are happiest when they are expressing their feelings through an art form—this is closely linked with the Emotional (Soul) plane.*

The character specifics

The letters in the above groups are further categorized into three character groups—these are generally labeled as Creative, Adaptable, and Grounded. Each character type works in conjunction with the four planes, as shown here:

	Mental	Physical	Emotional	Intuitive
Creative	A	E	O R I Z	K
Adaptable	H J N P	W	B S T X	F Q U Y
Grounded	G L	D M		C V

LETTER B
It can be seen from the character specifics chart that the letter "B" is associated with both Emotional and Adaptable attributes.

below *Both the Intuitive (Spirit) and Physical (Body) Planes of Expression can be associated with a love of the outdoors—for freedom and closeness to nature.*

The chart links the character specifics of the letters in the alphabet to the four planes, such that the letter "A," for instance, is linked with a blend of mental capacity and creative inspiration.

Creative

The letters A, E, I, K, O, R, and Z are not just associated with their listed planes, but also with creativity.

Adaptable

The letters B, F, H, J, N, P, Q, S, T, U, W, X, and Y are likewise linked with the mid-ground between creativity and being grounded.

Grounded

In a similar manner, the letters C, D, G, L, M, and V are considered to signify such attributes as practicality and balanced thoughtfulness.

Find your Planes of Expression

Your planes of expression can be identified using the chart above. My name, for example, can be examined thus:

William John Field

W	= Adaptable + Physical
I	= Creative + Emotional
L	= Grounded + Mental
L	= Grounded + Mental
I	= Creative + Emotional
A	= Creative + Mental
M	= Grounded + Physical
J	= Adaptable + Mental
O	= Creative + Emotional
H	= Adaptable + Mental
N	= Adaptable + Mental
F	= Adaptable + Intuitive
I	= Creative + Emotional
E	= Creative + Physical
L	= Grounded + Mental
D	= Grounded + Physical

The next stage is to look at the spread of planes and character specifics:

The Planes

Mental occurs 7 times
Physical occurs 4 times
Emotional occurs 4 times
Intuitive occurs once

The Character Specifics

Adaptable occurs 5 times
Creative occurs 6 times
Grounded occurs 5 times

So what does all this mean?

In order to make sense of the letter occurrences, it is necessary to look at the distributions of the various factors. As the planes are heavily biased to the mental aspects, it means that I am more of an analytical thinker than a spiritualist.

When viewed on their own, the three classes of character specifics are evenly spread, however, there is more to it than that:

There are four instances of Creative + Emotional
There are three instances of Grounded + Mental
There are two instances of Grounded + Physical
Adaptable is well distributed across all four planes.

This means that my Planes of Expression are centered around such things as innovation and imagination and that I am of a practical nature, whilst remaining well-balanced in most activities.

left *Your Planes of Expression may show that you are well suited to a particular avenue in life—this may be playing a musical instrument, or something completely different.*

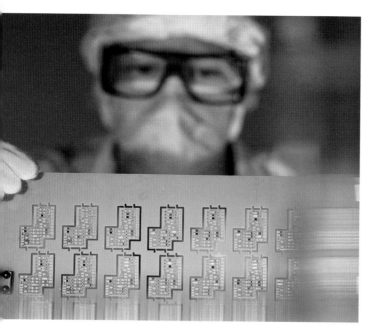

How to interpret your own Planes of Expression

When interpreting your own Planes of Expression, you need to look at the balance of each component, as shown here:

Mental

Few or no occurrences
Medium number of occurrences
Frequent occurrences

Associated characteristics

You work more by intuition than calculation
You work by feel and thought
Logic rules over all

Physical

Few or no occurrences
Medium number of occurrences
Frequent occurrences

Associated characteristics

You live in a dream world and are not competitive
You work well and get jobs finished
You work extremely hard and are very competitive

Emotional

Few or no occurrences
Medium number of occurrences
Frequent occurrences

Associated characteristics

You keep your feelings to yourself
You communicate your emotions well
Creative and caring, but headstrong

Intuitive

Few or no occurrences
Medium number of occurrences
Frequent occurrences

Associated characteristics

You are not very spiritual
You are open to spiritual matters
Spirituality dominates your life

above left *Achieving success in science or engineering usually requires a strong degree of mental capacity, as denoted by the Planes of Expression, together with a "Grounded" Character Specific.*

above right *Those who long for a life of travel and excitement may well show strong Creative attributes, however, there are no hard and fast rules.*

LETTER F The "F" is believed to be both Adaptable and Intuitive, and is linked with the mid-ground between creativity and being grounded.

THE SOUL URGE

top right *If you are able to satisfy your "Heart's Desires" or "Inner Dreams," you are likely to find a degree of inner peace.*

bottom right *When the Soul Urge is so inclined, the only way to achieve inner peace is to push the very limits of physical and mental endurance. Those who do not understand this often consider such individuals to be control freaks.*

The term "Soul Urge" is used in numerology to describe the things that make up your innermost desires as well as the things that you love or hate. It can also alternatively be referred to as "Heart's Desires" or "Inner Dreams." The various aspects from which it is comprised are revealed by the occurrence of the vowels that are used in your name. It is thought that if you are able to satisfy these desires, you are likely to find a degree of inner peace.

Find your Soul Urge / inner dreams

To find your Soul Urge, it is necessary to list the vowels in your name—that is, the letters A, E, I, O, and U, and then convert them into numeric values. These are then summed together and then reduced to a single digit.

My name, for example, can be examined thus:

The vowels in "William John Field" are I, I, A, O, I, and E.

The letters can be converted in number form using this chart:

1	2	3	4	5	6	7	8	9
A	B	C	D	E	F	G	H	I
J	K	L	M	N	O	P	Q	R
S	T	U	V	W	X	Y	Z	

I = **9**   A = **1**   O = **6**   E = **5**

The vowel "I" occurs three times, so: $3 \times 9 = $ **27**
There is one "A" $1 \times 1 = $ **1**
There is one "O" $1 \times 6 = $ **6**
There is one "E" $1 \times 5 = $ **5**

The total is: $27 + 1 + 6 + 5 = $ **39**.

$3 + 9 = $ **12**; $1 + 2 = $ **3**.

My Soul Urge number is therefore **3**.

Interpreting the Soul Urge number

The key aspects of the Soul Urge numbers are outlined here:

1 The number 1 signifies that you are very competitive, and that you are never happier than when you are winning at whatever task you have set yourself.

2 The number 2 suggests that you desperately seek peace and harmony, and that you will do whatever you can to avoid stressful situations. Whenever you are able to deliver peace to others, it gives you a great sense of well-being.

3 A Soul Urge number of 3 indicates being creative and gives you an enormous sense of satisfaction. This may be in the form of physical craftsmanship, or it may be found through artistic or literary pursuits.

4 The number 4 denotes a deep need for security —both in terms of money and your career. You gain satisfaction from clearing debts and building up financial savings.

5 The number 5 shows that you have a strong need to be in charge of your own destiny, and that anything that blocks this will generate feelings of frustration. Being free brings you satisfaction.

6 A Soul Urge number of 6 indicates that you need to feel loved and wanted, and as a result, you gain a lot of peace when your family and friends show their appreciation of you.

7 The number 7 shows that spiritual matters are very important to you, and that you find peace in quiet contemplation of the joys of life.

8 The number 8 is linked with a strong desire for material possessions and in gaining positions of authority in many different areas of your life. You gain satisfaction from long-term financial security and owning lots of pleasing things.

9 The number 9 is connected to idealism, compassion, and humanitarian pursuits. You feel fulfilled when you are able to do something to help others and go out of your way to be kind and considerate.

right A Soul Urge number of 6 is often associated with a need to feel loved and appreciated, and this often leads to a close link with family and friends.

THE PERSONALITY NUMBER

The consonants that are used in your name can be used to identify many aspects of your personality—consequently, this is known as your Personality Number. The character features revealed using this method are only those that you express to the outer world—in other words, only the ones that are near the surface. This can be important, however, as you can learn valuable lessons about how you are perceived by those around you.

Identify your Personality Number

To find your Personality Number, add the numerical value of the consonants of each of your names in the same manner as described earlier in the Expression and Soul Urge. Do not reduce the Master numbers 11 and 22 in the last stage when calculating the Personality Number. See Master Numbers on page 44 for an explanation.

My name, for example, can be examined thus: The consonants in "William John Field" are W, L, L, M, J, H, N, F, L, and D.

The letters can be converted in number form using this chart:

1	2	3	4	5	6	7	8	9
A	B	C	D	E	F	G	H	I
J	K	L	M	N	O	P	Q	R
S	T	U	V	W	X	Y	Z	

William
There is one "W" $1 \times 5 = 5$
The letter "L" occurs twice, so: $2 \times 3 = 6$
There is one "M" $1 \times 4 = 4$
            Total = 15; $1 + 5 = 6$

John
There is one "J" $1 \times 1 = 1$
There is one "H" $1 \times 8 = 8$
There is one "N" $1 \times 5 = 5$
            Total = 14; $1 + 4 = 5$

Field
There is one "F" $1 \times 6 = 6$
There is one "L" $1 \times 3 = 3$
There is one "D" $1 \times 4 = 4$
            Total = 13; $1 + 3 = 4$

Overall total = $6 + 5 + 4 = 15$; $1 + 5 = $ **6**

My Personality Number is therefore **6**—this can be interpreted using the listing opposite.

Keywords For The Personality Number

1 If a person with a Personality Number of 1 expresses themself in a positive manner, the outwardly apparent characteristics include such things as a flair for leadership and innovation. They also tend to show courage in their actions. However, if this aspect should steer toward the negative, then the individual may be perceived as being aggressive and unfeeling.

2 The positive aspects of a Personality Number of 2 generally result in an air of uncomplicated friendliness, sensitivity, and patience. Should the individual slide into negativity, however, they will come across as being uninteresting, and in extreme cases, thoroughly dull. They may well also exhibit varying degrees of shyness as well.

3 People with a Personality Number of 3 are usually optimistic, and have a refined but charming character. They are therefore seen by those around them as being interesting or attractive. The 3 is often given to romantic behavior. However, if the negative aspects take over, then the individual concerned may end up being seen as flighty as the result of spreading themselves too thinly.

4 The Personality Number 4 is often associated with such attributes as honesty and solidity. Such people are therefore seen by those around them as being trustworthy and efficient. Their striving for perfection can, however, tip over into negativity, and as a result they end up presenting themselves as being narrow-minded and lacking a sense of humor.

5 Those who have a Personality Number of 5 are generally witty, strong-minded, and innovative—as a result, they are often seen as being inspirational, and are usually socially popular. If they allow themselves to give in to the temptations of life, however, they can be prone to over-indulgence. This can lead others to see them as being irresponsible and self-centered.

6 The Personality Number 6 is linked to such caring attributes as compassion, a protective nature, and generosity. These characteristics can lead to the person being considered safe, humanitarian, or romantic. Where these attributes are not kept under control, however, the individual may be seen as being irresponsible with money or overly anxious.

7 A Personality Number of 7 is linked with such features as originality and intellectual depth. This can result in people with this number being perceived as studious and self-reliant. This often commands respect, but if the negative side rears its head, these individuals can become overly solemn and introspective. This can lead to perceptions of arrogance.

8 Individuals with the Personality Number 8 can demonstrate substantial enthusiasm, strength, and competence. Where these attributes are used positively, such people can establish good track records, which can result in them becoming very influential. The flip-side of this, however, is that if the negative aspects take over, they can become liable to anxiety and self-absorption.

9 Those with a Personality Number of 9 can display such positive aspects as charisma, elegance, and kindness, which can make them very popular in company. Where these attributes are left unchecked, however, the negative aspects can come to the fore, in which case the person can end up being seen as arrogant and superior. This can lead to unhappiness through isolation and loneliness.

right *When expressed in a positive manner, the Personality Number 4 is linked to honesty and solidity; however, the flip-side is a risk of becoming narrow-minded and lacking a sense of humor.*

BLENDING THE CORE ASPECTS

The Core Aspects of numerology—that is, the Life Path, Birth Day, Destiny Number, Soul Urge, and Personality can be combined using a Blending Table. This can then be used to reveal just what part each one is playing in your life.

Create a Blending Table

To create a Blending Table, it is first necessary to identify the values for the Core Aspects. Let us take the example of the famous scientist, Charles Robert Darwin, who was born on February 12th, 1809.

above *Although Charles Darwin became famous for his work on evolution, he was also a great humanitarian, taking great care of both his family and the poor who lived near him.*

His **Life Path Number** can be found from his Date of Birth (02–12–1809) – this sums up as below:

$0 + 2 + 1 + 2 + 1 + 8 + 0 + 9 =$ **23**; $2 + 3 =$ **5**

His Life Path Number = **5**.

His **Birth Day Number** is simply the day on which he was born – in this case, the 12th of the month.

His Birth Day Number = **12**.

His **Soul Urge Number** is found from the vowels in his name: Charles Robert Darwin. The conversion of the letters into numbers results in the following:

The vowel "I" occurs once, so: $1 \times 9 =$ **9**
There are two "A"s $2 \times 1 =$ **2**
There is one "O" $1 \times 6 =$ **6**
There are two "E"s $2 \times 5 =$ **10**

The total is: $9 + 2 + 6 + 10 =$ **27**. $2+7 =$ **9**

His Soul Urge Number = **9**.

His **Destiny Number** is found from the letters in his name:

Charles $= 3 + 8 + 1 + 9 + 3 + 5 + 1 =$ **30** $= 3 + 0 =$ **3**
Robert $= 9 + 6 + 2 + 5 + 9 + 2 =$ **33** (a Master Number*) $= 3 + 3 =$ **6**
Darwin $= 4 + 1 + 9 + 5 + 9 + 5 =$ **33** (a Master Number*) $= 3 + 3 =$ **6**

The total is: $3 + 6 + 6 =$ **15** $= 1 + 5 =$ **6**

His Destiny Number is **6**.

(* For more information on Master Numbers and how they work, see page 44.)

Darwin's **Personality Number** can be found thus:

The consonants in "Charles Robert Darwin" are C, H, R, L, S, R, B, R, T, D, R, W, and N

The letters can be converted to number form using this table:

1	2	3	4	5	6	7	8	9
A	B	C	D	E	F	G	H	I
J	K	L	M	N	O	P	Q	R
S	T	U	V	W	X	Y	Z	

Charles   There is one "C"   1 x 3 = **3**
There is one "H"   1 x 8 = **8**
There is one "R"   1 x 9 = **9**
There is one "L"   1 x 3 = **3**
There is one "S"   1 x 1 = **1**
Total = 24; 2 + 4 = **6**

above At his home, Down House in Kent, England, Darwin wrote On the Origin of Species, *one of the most influential books in human history.*

Robert   There are two "R"s   2 x 9 = **18**
There is one "B"   1 x 2 = **2**
There is one "T"   1 x 2 = **2**
Total = 22; 2 + 2 = **4**

Darwin   There is one "D"   1 x 4 = **4**
There is one "R"   1 x 9 = **9**
There is one "W"   1 x 5 = **5**
There is one "N"   1 x 5 = **5**
Total = 23; 2 + 3 = **5**

Overall total = 6 + 4 + 5 = **15**; 1 + 5 = **6**

His Personality Number is **6**.

DARWIN'S PERSONALITY NUMBER
The number 6 signifies a variety of positive aspects —including compassion, a protective nature, and generosity. Darwin was well known in his time as a humanitarian who cared for many people.

Now that Charles Darwin's five Core Aspects have been identified, they can be combined in a Blending Table:

Destiny

The Destiny or Expression Number reveals what opportunities may come along during a person's lifetime, and how they relate to others around them.

Destiny Number = 6

The positive aspects of the 6 are linked with such attributes as responsibility, balance, conscientiousness, compassion, honesty, creativity, and a loving nature. On the negative side, this number can be expressed through stubbornness, self-righteousness, and dominance.

right Darwin needed to display both the positive and the negative aspects of his Destiny Number of 6 to make the physical and intellectual leaps that came from his epic journey around the world in the ship "Beagle." He collected the tropical seashells seen here during his long journey.

Life Path

The Life Path Number represents how an individual's personal characteristics are likely to influence their journey through life, including the challenges they face and the lessons they learn as a result.

Life Path Number = 5

The positive aspects of the 5 are associated with idealism, adaptability, a love of adventure, and a natural curiosity. These people are often also compassionate, liberal, and communicate well. The negative aspects can lead to a lack of direction, self-indulgence, and indecision.

Birth Day

The Birth Day Number identifies what a person can make of their inherent attributes, as shown by the Life Path Number.

Birth Day Number = 12

A Birth Day Number of 12 is typically related to a number of positive characteristics, including the ability to communicate well, and having an innovative, artistic mind. Individuals with this number are also often practical and affectionate. If the negative side expresses itself, the person concerned may well become superficial with a moody, oversensitive outlook.

Soul Urge

The Soul Urge Number reveals a person's innermost desires as well as the things they love or hate.

Soul Urge Number = 9

The number 9 is connected to idealism, compassion, and humanitarian pursuits. You feel fulfilled when you are able to do something to help others.

Personality

The Personality Number identifies many of the more visible aspects of an individual's personality.

Personality Number = 6

The number 6 is linked to such positive caring attributes as compassion, a protective nature, and generosity. Where these attributes are not kept under control, however, the individual may be seen as being irresponsible with money or overly anxious.

The Blending Table

The next stage is to interpret the chart—this is a process which requires a significant amount of consideration and intuition as there are no set rules. In essence, what you are trying to do is understand just how the Core Aspects that you find in the Blending Table are likely to work with one another in combination. Someone with attributes that all fit well with each other may be content in life; however, it can also mean that they lack the fire to achieve anything worthwhile. Likewise, antagonistic features can work for or against the bigger picture. When deciphering the Blending Table, it is important to remember that what you are looking for is a constructive outcome. A report filled solely with doom and gloom will do no-one any favors, so try to identify where lessons can be learned. This can put a positive slant on things, and it is then down to the individual concerned as to whether they are prepared to put the work in to move onward and upward. Although it may seem to be a difficult process to get right, it is one that becomes easier as experience is gained.

THE CORE ASPECTS
The Core Aspects mesh together like mechanical cogs to form a bigger picture.

above *An individual with a balanced personality can make all manner of connections in life.*
left *A Life Path Number of 5 is associated with people who demonstrate idealism, adaptability, and compassion—they also tend to communicate well, and so are well-suited to diplomatic affairs.*

Aim to interpret the Blending Table in a positive manner.

HARMONIOUS & DISCORDANT ASPECTS

The five Core Aspects of numerology—that is, the Destiny Number, Life Path, Birth Day, Soul Urge, and Personality—can work with (Harmonious) or against (Discordant) one another. For example, someone who wanted to undertake a long course of study might find that their Soul Urge was compatible with slow, steady learning, but that their Personality Number indicated a poor focus. Such a combination would be considered Discordant, and under such circumstances, it would be wise for such a person to plan carefully before embarking on activities like protracted academic exercises. Another person with a similar Soul Urge, however, could find that their Personality Number revealed a high degree of dedication, consistency and a love of hard work. In such a case, their Core Aspects would be considered Harmonious, and they would be ideally suited to the task. It is therefore important to ensure that the ways that your Core Aspects interact are understood so that you can get the most out of your life. Even the most conflicted attributes can be worked around if there is the will to do so!

Find out if your Core Concepts are Harmonious or Discordant

As with the interpretation of the Blending Table, working out which of the Core Aspects are likely to result in a beneficial character profile, and which do the reverse, is a subjective matter. The more experience a practitioner has, the easier the process becomes. The primary characteristics of each of the numbers 1–9 can be seen in the table opposite. By comparing the attributes of a person's Core Aspects with the keywords listed, it is possible to figure out which ones are likely to work in harmony, and which are likely to be discordant.

right When the Harmonious Aspects combine in a positive manner, you will not only be able to achieve inner peace, but those around you will find your calmness especially appealing. Should the aspects be Discordant, however, you may have to work much harder to achieve your goals.

A summary of the keywords for the Harmonious & Discordant Aspects

1 Innovation. Self-reliance. Reliability. Leadership. Organization.

2 Creativity. Unreliability. Intellectual. Over-sensitive. Humanitarian. Insecure.

3 Drive. Material success. Spirituality. Compassion. Organization. Morality. Harmony.

4 Open-minded. Sensitive. Shirks convention. Innovative. Curious.

5 Organization. Intelligent. Adaptability. Material success. Strength. Communication.

above *Examining your Core Aspects for Harmonious and Discordant attributes may well show that romance is on the agenda.*

6 Romance. Luxury. Spirituality. Harmony. Domesticity. Happiness.

7 Creativity. Imagination. Spirituality. Innovative. Artistic.

8 Spirituality. Travel. Introversion. Management. Shirks convention. Extremism.

9 Ambitious. Dynamic. Leadership. Aggressive. Confident.

THE NUMBER INTENSITY

Practitioners of numerology use what is known as either "The Intensification of Numbers" or "Special Traits" to discover some of the more deeply hidden personal characteristics. Some do this based on the appearance or non-appearance of the numbers 1–9 in the birth date. Others also use the frequency of the letters A–Z in the full birth name. When a number is repeated more times than the average, it signifies that the attributes for that number are magnified. When they occur less frequently—especially if they are missing altogether—the negative aspects are expressed instead. This information is often used to determine which areas of a person's life need to be further developed or given special consideration.

It is worth noting that the average number of times a certain digit appears changes with time—for instance, in the second millennium, where all years begin with the number "2," the frequency of appearance of this number is going to be significantly higher than during the first millennium, in which they all began with the number "1."

Reveal the Special Traits due to Number Intensity.

Number Intensity—Names

Let us illustrate the methods used in revealing the special traits by taking the example of Franklin Delano Roosevelt, the 32nd President of the USA, who lived from January 30th, 1882 to April 12th, 1945.

The letters can be converted to number form using this table:

1	2	3	4	5	6	7	8	9
A	B	C	D	E	F	G	H	I
J	K	L	M	N	O	P	Q	R
S	T	U	V	W	X	Y	Z	

Using the letter-to-number chart above, it is possible to examine the ratio of letters/numbers:

FRANKLIN DELANO ROOSEVELT
6 9 1 5 2 3 9 5   4 5 3 1 5 6   9 6 6 1 5 4 5 3 2

The frequency of number occurrences in F. D. Roosevelt's name can be seen here:

1 = 3 times	**4** = 2 times	**7** = missing
2 = 2 times	**5** = 6 times	**8** = missing
3 = 3 times	**6** = 4 times	**9** = 3 times

The average number of times that a number occurs in a name can be seen here:

Number:	1	2	3	4	5	6	7	8	9
Average occurrence:	3	2	1	1	3	1	1	1	3

The chart shown here reveals that the numbers 3, 5, and 6 have an above-average appearance, and so are the most significant. The chart below shows the numbers and their associated keywords. History shows that he was an original thinker, who expressed creativity and intellect. He was a well-traveled man, who spoke several languages. He is also known to have had several affairs, in spite of being married; these aspects —travel, romance, and intellect—are seen in the number 5. He also had driving ambition and a deep sense of duty—these are seen in the qualities of the number 6.

Number Intensity—birth dates
A similar process can be performed on the birth date—let us take the example of King Henry VIII, who lived from June 28th, 1491 to January 28th, 1547:

This equates to: 06 28 1491 = 6 28 1491

The frequency of number occurrences in King Henry VIII's birth date can be seen here:

1 = twice	**4** = once	**7** = missing
2 = once	**5** = missing	**8** = once
3 = missing	**6** = once	**9** = once

Since he has more occurrences of the number 1 than any other digit, this is his Number Intensity. It can be seen from the Letter and Number Intensity Chart that this number is particularly associated with leadership, conviction, and ambition. These are all attributes that helped to make him such a notorious monarch.

MONEY The pursuit of money can cause people to make poor judgments. The Number Intensities can be used to help identify deeply hidden characteristics.

Keywords for the Letter and Number Intensity

Letter	Number	Associated Keywords
A - J - S	1	Leadership. Conviction. Ambition.
B - K - T	2	Harmony. Spirituality. Diplomacy.
C - L - U	3	Originality. Creativity. Happiness.
D - M - V	4	Organization. Management.
E - N - W	5	Intellect. Romance. Travel.
F - O - X	6	Creativity. Duty. Ambition.
G - P - Y	7	Intellect. Spirituality. Respect. Self-sufficiency.
H - Q - Z	8	Influential. Effective. Competent.
I - R	9	Compassionate. Humanitarian. Charismatic.

MASTER NUMBERS

Master Numbers

below Clint Eastwood, star of so many classic movies, was born Clinton Eastwood. On examination, it can be seen that his Life Path Number is 22—one of the Master Numbers.
right The Master Number 11—the psychic's number—is associated with many positive attributes, including sensitivity, idealism, charisma, and leadership, as well as negative ones, such as a lack of self-confidence.

There are nine basic numbers used in numerology—these are, of course, 1–9. Alongside them are—depending on which convention you use—a series of so-called "Master Numbers." The most widely used system considers these to be the numbers 11 and 22, the other most common method also includes the number 33. There are other, less widespread methods which also include 44, 55, and 66. Unlike other multiple digit numbers, the Master Numbers are not reduced to their most basic single digit form. As with many other aspects of the subject, some practitioners believe that these have special spiritual significance, whereas others do not. Each of the Master Numbers has its own set of characteristics—these are shown in the keyword chart opposite.

How to reveal the Master Numbers

Let us take the example of Clint Eastwood (born May 31st, 1930)—whose full birth name is Clinton Eastwood:

The letters are converted using this chart:

1	2	3	4	5	6	7	8	9
A	B	C	D	E	F	G	H	I
J	K	L	M	N	O	P	Q	R
S	T	U	V	W	X	Y	Z	

Clinton = 3 + 3 + 9 + 5 + 2 + 6 + 5 = **33**
Eastwood = 5 + 1 + 1 + 2 + 5 + 6 + 6 + 4 = **30**

This shows that his first name corresponds to the Master Number **33**.

Likewise, his Birth Number is also a Master Number—this can be seen here:

May 31st, 1930 = 31 05 1930
= 3 + 1 + 0 + 5 + 1 + 9 + 3 = **22**.

Therefore his Life Path Number is **22**, a Master Number which is considered to be the most powerful of all numbers.

Master Numbers

A Keyword Summary For Master Numbers

The Master Number 11 is associated with:
Positive: Perception. Sensitivity. Idealism. Charisma. Leadership. Inspiration. Energy. Spirituality.
Negative: Anxiety. Lack of self-confidence. Impracticality. Instability. Self-destruction.
The **11** is the psychic's number.

The Master Number 22 is associated with:
Positive: Goal achievement. Perception. Practicality. Organized. Self-discipline. Idealism. Leadership. Self-confidence.
Negative: Avoidance of life's possibilities and responsibilities.
The **22** is the most powerful of all numbers.

The Master Number 33 is associated with:
Positive: Spirituality. Honesty. Commitment. Drive. Knowledge. Understanding.
Negative: A propensity to becoming over-demanding.
The **33** is the most influential of all numbers.

above The 22 is the most powerful of all numbers. It is often called the Master Builder. The 22 can turn the most ambitious of dreams into reality and is potentially the most successful of all numbers.

Unlike other multiple digit numbers, the Master Numbers are not reduced to their most basic single digit form.

THE GROWTH NUMBER

opposite page *When the Growth Number coincides with one or more Core Aspects, a high degree of personal balance can be achieved, leading to inner peace and a sense of overall harmony.*

An individual's Growth Number is found by converting the letters in the first name into their numeric equivalents, and then adding them together. It is thought to be a guide to many deep issues as the first name is such a personal thing. It is considered especially significant if the number is the same as that for any of the Core Aspects, in which case it reinforces them.

This can be seen with the example of the famous movie actor Charlton Heston (October 4th, 1923 to April 5th, 2008)—who was born "John Charles Carter." His growth number is 2, as can be seen here:

John: J = 1   O = 6   H = 8   N = 5

Since: $1 + 6 + 8 + 5 = $ **20**, and: $2 + 0 = $ **2**, his Growth Number is **2**.

This coincides with his Life Path Number, which is also 2, as can be seen from his birth date:

October 4th, 1923
$= 1 + 0 + 4 + 1 + 9 + 2 + 3 = $ **20**; $2 + 0 = $ **2**

Heston's Growth Number therefore reinforces the attributes revealed by his Life Path Number (see pages 22–3).

THE POWER OF 2
Heston's Growth Number and Life Path Number are both 2—this reinforces such attributes as his communication skills and idealism.

left *The actor Charlton Heston was the star of many famous movies, including* El Cid, The Ten Commandments, Ben Hur, *and* Planet of the Apes.

The Growth Number

THE PINNACLES

The Pinnacles are an important concept in numerology, and are used to characterize the four main stages in life, much like the seasons of the year. The First Pinnacle is usually considered to last from birth until anywhere between the ages of 27 and 35. The Second Pinnacle then takes over for nine years, after which the next nine years make up the Third Pinnacle. The final phase—the Fourth Pinnacle, lasts until death. Analysis of the pinnacles provides information that can be used for predictive purposes, or to highlight factors that can be used to learn valuable lessons. This information, which is derived from your birth date, can be used to highlight the various paths within your life.

For example, we can discern The Pinnacles for the great movie star, Steve McQueen (born Terrence Steven McQueen, March 24th, 1930, died November 7th, 1980).

The first stage is to reduce each part of his birth date to a single digit:

Birth Date = March 24th, 1930
Month Number = **3**
Day Number = 24 = 2 + 4 = **6**
Year Number = 1930 = 1 + 9 + 3 + 0 = 13;
$$1 + 3 = 4$$

The First Pinnacle is found by adding the Day Number and the Month Number:

The Day Number = **6**, and the Month Number = **3**, thus the First Pinnacle = 6 + 3 = **9**.

The Second Pinnacle is found by adding the Day Number and the Year Number:

The Day Number = 6, and the Year Number = 4, thus the Second Pinnacle = 6 + 4 = 10; 1 + 0 = **1**.

The Third Pinnacle is found by adding the First and Second Pinnacles together:

The First Pinnacle = 9, the Second Pinnacle = 1, thus the Third Pinnacle = 9 + 1 = 10; 1 + 0 = **1**.

The Fourth Pinnacle is found by adding the Month Number and the Year Number:

The Month Number = 3, Year Number = 4, thus the Fourth Pinnacle = 3 + 4 = **7**.

The Pinnacles are used to characterize the four main stages in life, much like the seasons of the year.

A Summary of the Keywords for the Habit Challenges

1 The Number of Leadership
This number is associated with the following Habit Challenges: A lack of self-confidence. Impatience. Becoming overly entrenched and aggressive to those who question your standpoint. Acting without thinking about the consequences. Over-dominance.

2 The Number of Diplomacy
This number is associated with the following Habit Challenges: A difficulty in making decisions. Becoming over-sensitive to any forms of criticism and an over-dependence on others in even the simplest situations.

3 The Number of Communication
This number is associated with the following Habit Challenges: Becoming too thinly spread, with a consequent difficulty in maintaining focus. Anxiety common.

4 The Number of Structure
This number is associated with the following Habit Challenges: A lack of structure, with a consequent lack of organization. A fear of making decisions. Blinkered vision. A risk of being aggressive to others.

5 The Number of Adventure
This number is associated with the following Habit Challenges: A fear of making decisions. Acting without thinking about the consequences. A lack of focus and attention to detail. On top of the game one day, poor the next.

6 The Number of Duty
This number is associated with the following Habit Challenges: Remote emotions. A risk of becoming self-centered. A lack of structure, with a consequent lack of organization. Shirking responsibility.

7 The Number of Originality
This number is associated with the following Habit Challenges: Becoming over-sensitive to criticism and yet very critical of others. Shallowness. Jealousy. There is a distinct possibility of becoming overly introverted, with the consequent risk of loneliness.

8 The Number of Implementation
This number is associated with the following Habit Challenges: A lack of structure, with a consequent lack of organization. A risk of being aggressive to others. A lack of direction and/or drive. Asking too much of others.

9 The Number of Humanity
This number is associated with the following Habit Challenges: Remote emotions. Over-dominance. There is a distinct possibility of becoming overly introverted, with the consequent risk of loneliness. A lack of direction. Over-sensitivity.

above *The number 9 is often connected with such Habit Challenges as emotional remoteness, loneliness, and an over-bearing personality.*

THE MATURITY NUMBER

The Maturity Number is used in numerology to reveal what sort of character you are likely to have later in life. It is found by adding together two of your Core Aspects—your Life Path Number and your Destiny Number. Alternative names for this attribute are "Reality Number" and "Ultimate Goal Number"—they all mean the same thing. The overall result sums up the lessons learned in the early and middle parts of life, and indicates how the lessons learned may be used. In essence, it highlights the wisdom a person has gained on their journey since birth.

above *The archetypal cowboy John Wayne was the star of countless movies and a hero to his many fans and admirers all over the world.*

As an illustration, let us examine John Wayne's (May 26th, 1907—June 11th, 1979) Maturity Number:

Firstly, it is important to remember that John Wayne's real name was Marion Michael Morrison, and that this is what must be used.

His Life Path Number is found from his birth date:

Birth date: May 26th, 1907

May = 0 + 5 = **5**
26 = 2 + 6 = **8**
1907 = 17 = 1 + 7 = **8**

5 + 8 + 8 = 21; 2 + 1 = **3**

John Wayne's Life Path Number is therefore **3**.

His Destiny Number is found from his full birth name:
Full birth name: Marion Michael Morrison

M A R I O N
4+1+9+9+6+5 = **34**

M I C H A E L
4+9+3+8+1+5+3 = **33**

M O R R I S O N
4+6+9+9+9+1+6+5 = **49**

34 + 33 + 49 = **116**
116 = 1 + 1 + 6 = **8**
John Wayne's Destiny Number is therefore **8**.

John Wayne's Maturity Number is then found by adding his Life Path Number of 3 to his Destiny Number, which is 8:

Life Path Number of **3** + Destiny Number of **8**; Maturity Number = **11** (See the Keyword Summary on page 45.)

The Maturity Number is concerned with the nature of a person's character in their later life.

Keywords for the Maturity Number

1 A person with a Maturity Number of 1 who takes the trouble to learn from life's lessons will benefit in their later years from a fulfilled character. This will be rich in many positive aspects. Where life's lessons were not taken on board, however, the negative aspects can surface, and they may end up as being dogmatic, self-centered, and ultimately, lonely.

2 A Maturity Number of 2 signifies that an individual's life goals may include such positive attributes as developing an advanced degree of human understanding and diplomacy. If this is not channeled properly, however, the person concerned may end up by becoming over-sensitive.

3 In later years, an individual with a Maturity Number of 3 may well get involved in various out-going behaviors. These often include very sociable lifestyles that might center around the arts. While all this can be a very good thing, should the individuals concerned fail to understand life's lessons, they can easily find themselves getting too caught up in the downsides. This can be expressed as shallowness, self-indulgence, and vanity.

4 A Maturity Number of 4 shows that the person concerned can derive deep satisfaction from taking on tasks and seeing them through to completion. This draws on a variety of skills learned on life's journey. If this is not held in check, however, the individual risks ending up being narrow-minded and dogmatic.

5 A Maturity Number of 5 is typically associated with people who have experienced many adventures during their life. Those who manage to learn positive lessons from their trials can hope to spend their mature years enjoying peace and satisfaction. On the other hand, those individuals who fail to make the most of themselves earlier on are likely to end up bored and resentful.

6 A Maturity Number of 6 is often linked with people who display such attributes as idealism and spirituality. Those individuals who manage to benefit in a positive manner from the challenges they encounter on life's journey can look forward to being involved in many years of family or other social activity. The downside is that people with a Maturity Number of 6 who did not learn how the world works can end up as being too cautious and overly idealistic.

7 People with a Maturity Number of 7 often have studious and self-reliant characters, and this can result in professional or other intellectual careers. Those who take life's lessons on board can develop a significant level of intuition and understanding where other people are concerned. This can lead to such individuals seeking the space to contemplate deeply philosophical matters in their later years. If, however, they failed to comprehend the challenges that faced them in the earlier part of their lives, they risk becoming very introverted and lonely.

8 A Maturity Number of 8 is usually associated with people who have spent much of their lives striving for career progression and/or the acquisition of material possessions. Those who manage to achieve this can look forward to spending their later years in a satisfied and secure manner. This is easily displaced, however, if the negative aspects are allowed to flourish, with greed and the ego taking over.

9 A Maturity Number of 9 can be linked with individuals who have a compassionate and creative nature. Such people often choose careers where they are exposed to a variety of life's challenges. Those who learn from these lessons can spend their later years benefiting from all the wisdom they have accumulated, and using this for humanitarian purposes. Those who chose not to learn from what life put before them, however, are likely to end up being seen as arrogant and remote. This can result in a deep sense of loneliness.

THE PINNACLES

opposite page Here, youngsters in their First Pinnacle are fortunate enough to gain from the life experience of someone in a later Pinnacle.

The Pinnacles are an important concept in numerology, and are used to characterize the four main stages in life, much like the seasons of the year. The First Pinnacle is usually considered to last from birth until anywhere between the ages of 27 and 35. The Second Pinnacle then takes over for nine years, after which the next nine years make up the Third Pinnacle. The final phase—the Fourth Pinnacle, lasts until death. Analysis of the pinnacles provides information that can be used for predictive purposes, or to highlight factors that can be used to learn valuable lessons. This information, which is derived from your birth date, can be used to highlight the various paths within your life.

For example, we can discern The Pinnacles for the great movie star, Steve McQueen (born Terrence Steven McQueen, March 24th, 1930, died November 7th, 1980).

The first stage is to reduce each part of his birth date to a single digit:

Birth Date = March 24th, 1930
Month Number = **3**
Day Number = 24 = 2 + 4 = **6**
Year Number = 1930 = 1 + 9 + 3 + 0 = 13;
$$1 + 3 = \mathbf{4}$$

The First Pinnacle is found by adding the Day Number and the Month Number:

The Day Number = **6**, and the Month Number = **3**, thus the First Pinnacle = 6 + 3 = **9**.

The Second Pinnacle is found by adding the Day Number and the Year Number:

The Day Number = 6, and the Year Number = 4, thus the Second Pinnacle = 6 + 4 = 10; 1 + 0 = **1**.

The Third Pinnacle is found by adding the First and Second Pinnacles together:

The First Pinnacle = 9, the Second Pinnacle = 1, thus the Third Pinnacle = 9 + 1 = 10; 1 + 0 = **1**.

The Fourth Pinnacle is found by adding the Month Number and the Year Number:

The Month Number = 3, Year Number = 4, thus the Fourth Pinnacle = 3 + 4 = **7**.

right Steve McQueen was one of the greatest movie stars of all time, appearing in such classics as The Great Escape and Bullitt. He was truly one of a kind—a passionate racer and collector of motorcycles and cars, he tragically died from cancer at the relatively young age of 50.

The Pinnacles are used to characterize the four main stages in life, much like the seasons of the year.

MATERIAL SUCCESS The desire for material success is linked with the numbers 5 and 8 in the Second and Third Pinnacles, and 3 and 5 in the Fourth Pinnacle.

Second and Third Pinnacles

1 Strongly-driven. Self-reliance. Leadership.
2 Patience. Hard-working. Intellectual.
3 Creativity. Artistic. Compassion. Sensitivity.
4 Drive. Hard-working. Innovative.
5 Need for independence. Adaptability. Material success.
6 Diplomatic. Responsible. Domesticity.
7 Spiritual. Introverted. Artistic.
8 Driven. Material success.
9 Dynamic. Humanitarian. Compassionate. Idealistic.

Summary of the Keywords for the Pinnacles

First Pinnacle

1 Innovation. Leadership. Self-reliance.
2 Over-sensitivity. Highly strung. Poor communication.
3 Artistic. Creative. Drive. Fun before work.
4 Highly-motivated. Hard working. Innovative.
5 Original. Independent. Organization. Impulsive.
6 Dutiful. Responsible. Romantic.
7 Spiritual. Lonely. Artistic.
8 Logical. Original. Introverted.
9 Compassionate. Humanitarian. Idealist. Confident.

Fourth Pinnacle

1 Duty. Leadership. Originality. Self-reliance.
2 Harmony. Patience. Compassion. Intellectual.
3 Sociable. Active. Material success. Creativity.
4 Hard-working. Responsible. Shirks convention.
5 Material success. Drive. Organization.
6 Home-loving. Luxury. Happiness.
7 Spiritual. Introverted. Imaginative.
8 Drive. Leadership. Management.
9 Humanitarian. Dynamic. Compassion.

THE CHALLENGES

Everyone faces difficult periods in their life, and in numerology these are referred to as the "Challenges." They are usually considered to occur in periods of nine years in tandem with the Pinnacles. Some practitioners believe that there are three different kinds—two Sub-Challenges, and one primary event which is known as the Main Life Challenge; others, however, add a fourth. These are essentially hurdles which we must overcome if we are to succeed in continuing life's journey. Those who do so successfully learn vital lessons, and these can be carried forward for future use. The Challenges are therefore an important part of developing as a fulfilled person, and each is related to the birth date.

right *Life has a way of placing many different hurdles in our way, and sometimes these can be incredibly difficult to overcome. Those who have the will and stamina to succeed, however, can usually find a way to achieve this.*

The First Sub-Challenge

The First Sub-Challenge is found from the Birth Date, with the Month Number being subtracted from the Day Number. Let us take the example of Charlie Chaplin (his full name is Sir Charles Spencer Chaplin), who lived from April 16th, 1889 to December 25th, 1977.

In this case, the birth date of April 16th, 1889 works out thus:

Birth Date: April 16th, 1889

Day Number: 16; 1 + 6 = **7**

Month Number: **4**

First Sub-Challenge Number = 7 − 4 = **3**

above *Life is full of challenges, and there are times when we all feel just like a cog in a wheel. However, like Charlie Chaplin playing the plucky underdog, with the help of the numerological Sub-Challenges we can all rise up and face the difficulties that beset us in life.*

The Second Sub-Challenge

The Second Sub-Challenge is found in a very similar manner, with the Day Number being subtracted from the Year Number.

Birth Date: April 16th, 1889

Year Number: 1 + 8 + 8 + 9 = 26; 2 + 6 = **8**

Day Number: 16; 1 + 6 = **7**

Second Sub-Challenge Number = 8 − 7 = **1**

CHARLIE CHAPLIN
Sir Charles Spencer Chaplin was one of the world's most loved, famous, and widely imitated comedians of all time.

The Challenges II

The Third or Main Life Challenge

The Main Life Challenge is derived by subtracting the Second Sub-Challenge from the First Sub-Challenge.

Since the First Sub-Challenge Number = **3**, and the Second Sub-Challenge Number = **1**:

The Main Life Challenge = 3 − 1 = **2**.

The Fourth Sub-Challenge

The Fourth Sub-Challenge is found by subtracting the Month Number from the Year Number.

Birth Date: April 16th, 1889
Year Number: 1 + 8 + 8 + 9 = 26; 2 + 6 = **8**
Month Number: **4**
The Fourth Sub-Challenge = 8 − 4 = **4**.

FEW SHOW "0" The Challenge Number 0 is the figure of indecision. The lesson to be learned is that of believing in yourself and taking charge of your own destiny.

below *Sometimes the challenges are emotional ones, but in the real world, they can also be of a very practical form.*

above *Life can sometimes appear to be an uphill struggle. Those who find the energy to prevail will achieve far more inner peace than those who give up on the way.*

Everyone faces difficult periods in their life—these are referred to as the "Challenges."

The Challenge Numbers

0 This is the number of indecision—that is, you are likely to allow your emotions to get in the way when faced with a series of choices. The lesson to be learned is that of believing in yourself and taking charge of your own destiny.

1 This is the number of judgment—your challenge in life will be to control your actions in difficult situations, and handle your affairs in a more diplomatic manner. The lesson to be learned is that of standing up for yourself when other people or situations put you under pressure.

2 The 2 Challenge Number signifies a sensitive disposition, and the main challenge that you will have to overcome is that of learning how to communicate your position to others in a manner that is both assertive and constructive.

3 The number 3 denotes a tendency for introversion and a fear of criticism. The lesson to be learned is that of making the effort to lead rather than follow, to communicate, and to be sociable when you would rather hide away from the limelight.

4 The challenge here is to find the right balance in life between work and play, and the lesson to be learned is to understand that some things are more important than simply enjoying yourself. In so doing, it is also necessary that you manage your time so that you finish the jobs you start.

5 The Challenge Number 5 indicates that given the chance, you will attempt to avoid any responsibility that comes your way. The lesson to be learned is that of distinguishing between unnecessary burdens and taking on those that you should accept.

6 A Challenge Number 6 is associated with an inner need for reaching high goals, especially those that involve some form of learning. The lesson to be taken on board is that of achieving a good balance between helping others and being seen as interfering or over-bearing.

7 The number 7 is linked with communication issues —especially with a tendency to repress one's feelings or to criticize others. The lesson here is to learn how to demonstrate affection and appreciation for those around you.

8 The Challenge Number 8 is usually considered to reveal a dependence on material possessions or social status. The lesson to be learned is that of accepting that the simple things in life such as honesty and affection are more important than the objects that money can buy.

above *The Challenge Number 8 can reveal a dependence on material possessions or social status—the lesson is to accept the simple things in life, such as honesty and affection.*

THE LIFE PATH PERIODS

far right The three Life Path Periods begin with the early phase.

In numerology, someone who lives out the full term of a natural life is considered to have gone through three Life Path Periods—these make up the early, main, and late years. This concept is effectively an extension to the previously discussed Life Path (see page 23), and when applied can reveal a number of further features. It is entirely possible that these will result in inconsistencies when related to previous readings which were based solely on the Life Path Number. Under such circumstances, it is probably best to go back over the whole process in order to ensure that nothing was misinterpreted.

below Frank Sinatra was born Francis Albert Sinatra on December 12th, 1915, and died on May 14th, 1998.

How to identify the Life Path Periods

The three Life Path Periods are derived from the full birth date—the first being denoted by the month of birth, the second by the day of birth, and the third by the year. The First Life Path Period begins at birth and continues until around the age of 28. As such, it covers childhood, the teenage years, and the first stages of becoming an adult. It is this period, therefore, that forms the foundations for later life. The exact end point of the first period is determined by astrological factors. After this, the Second Life Path Period takes over and lasts until the person concerned reaches around 56 years of age. It is the most important stage, when most of life's achievements are reached, and families fostered. The Third Life Path Period is made up of years when the accumulated knowledge and wisdom can be put to good effect. It is worth noting that the shift from one Life Path Period to the next is typically a very gradual process, and so is usually imperceptible to the subject.

To illustrate the principle, let us take the example of Frank Sinatra, who was born Francis Albert Sinatra on December 12th, 1915, and died on May 14th, 1998.

The first stage is to identify his Life Path Number, which is determined by the sum of the birth date:

December 12th, 1915 = 12 – 12 – 1915 =
1 + 2 + 1 + 2 + 1 + 9 + 1 + 5 = 22; since this is a Master Number, it is not reduced any further.

Frank Sinatra's Life Path Number is therefore **22**. As there is no 22nd month, he did not have a First Life Path Period.

The start of his Second Life Path Period is more complicated to determine. The first component

The three Life Path Periods are derived from the full birth date—the first being denoted by the month of birth, the second by the day of birth, and the third by the year.

is finding which was the closest year to his 28th birthday, where he had a Personal Year Number value of 1. In his case, this turns out to be 1948, as can be seen here:

Birth Month Number + Birth Day Number =
12 + 12 = 24; 2 + 4 = **6**.

In 1948 = 1 + 9 + 4 + 8 = 22; 2 + 2 = **4**

6 + 4 = 10; 1 + 0 = **1**, thus Frank Sinatra had a Personal Year Number of 1 in 1948.

His Second Life Path Period therefore started on New Year's Day 1948, when he was 33 years old.

In a similar manner, his Third Life Path Period started on New Year's Day of the year with a Personal Year Number of 1, that is closest to his 56th birthday. This turns out to be 1975, as can be seen here:

Birth Month Number + Birth Day Number =
12 + 12 = 24; 2 + 4 = **6**.

In 1975 = 1 + 9 + 7 + 5 = 22; 2 + 2 = **4**

6 + 4 = 10; 1 + 0 = **1**, thus Frank Sinatra had a Personal Year Number of **1** in 1975 (see page 27).

FRANK SINATRA Frank Sinatra started his career as a musician, but later also became an acclaimed actor, for which he won several awards. Examples of his work include *Guys and Dolls*, *From Here to Eternity*, *The Man with the Golden Arm*, and *High Society*.

THE ESSENCES

JIMI HENDRIX The legendary musician Jimi Hendrix (November 27th, 1942– September 18th, 1970) was born "Johnny Allen Hendrix."

Another way of analyzing your personal characteristics through numerology is via what are known as "The Essences." These use the number equivalents of the letters in your full birth name to highlight certain attributes of your personality—this is done for each year of your life, and should be considered in conjunction with the Personal Year reading.

The Essences can be used to highlight certain attributes of your personality.

right *Hendrix, who was known for his wild stage performances, was one of the most influential rock guitarists of all time.*

How to perform an Essence Reading

Determining the Essence Numbers for each year of your life is a straightforward, but somewhat lengthy process. It involves creating a chart that extends into the future as far as you think sensible. To start off, you take the initial letters of your first, middle, and last names, convert them to their equivalent number values, and then reduce these to a single digit. This figure then represents the Essences for the first year of your life. Each letter is then repeated for the years that follow—the number of times this occurs is determined by its numeric value. For instance, if the letter in question is "D" (which has the value 4), then it is repeated four times. This can be seen in the example chart opposite which has been compiled for the legendary musician, Jimi Hendrix (November 27th, 1942 –September 18th, 1970), whose Full Birth Name was "Johnny Allen Hendrix." The names are simply repeated if you run out of letters.

Essence chart for "Johnny Allen Hendrix"

Year	Age	Transits (First,	Middle,	Last)	Number Values			Essence
1942	0–1	J	A	H	1	1	8	10 / 1
1943	1–2	O	L	H	6	3	8	17 / 8
1944	2–3	O	L	H	6	3	8	17 / 8
1945	3–4	O	L	H	6	3	8	17 / 8
1946	4–5	O	L	H	6	3	8	17 / 8
1947	5–6	O	L	H	6	3	8	17 / 8
1948	6–7	O	L	H	6	3	8	17 / 8
1949	7–8	H	E	H	8	5	8	21 / 3
1950	8–9	H	E	E	8	5	5	18 / 9
1951	9–10	H	E	E	8	5	5	18 / 9
1952	10–11	H	E	E	8	5	5	18 / 9
1953	11–12	H	E	E	8	5	5	18 / 9
1954	12–13	H	N	E	8	5	5	18 / 9
1955	13–14	H	N	N	8	5	5	18 / 9
1956	14–15	H	N	N	8	5	5	18 / 9
1957	15–16	N	N	N	5	5	5	15 / 6
1958	16–17	N	N	N	5	5	5	15 / 6
1959	17–18	N	A	N	5	1	5	11 / 2
1960	18–19	N	L	D	5	3	4	12 / 3
1961	19–20	N	L	D	5	3	4	12 / 3
1962	20–21	N	L	D	5	3	4	12 / 3
1963	21–22	N	L	D	5	3	4	12 / 3
1964	22–23	N	L	R	5	3	9	17 / 8
1965	23–24	N	L	R	5	3	9	17 / 8
1966	24–25	N	E	R	5	5	9	19 /10/ 1
1967	25–26	Y	E	R	7	5	9	21 / 3
1968	26–27	Y	E	R	7	5	9	21 / 3
1969	27–28	Y	E	R	7	5	9	21 / 3
1970	28–29	Y	E	R	7	5	9	21 / 3

Number of Years	1	2	3	4	5	6	7	8	9
	A	B	C	D	E	F	G	H	I
	J	K	L	M	N	O	P	Q	R
	S	T	U	V	W	X	Y	Z	-

Number equivalence chart for each of the letters

What the Essence Numbers mean

1 The Essence Number 1 is associated with personal development and the possibility of significantly improved opportunities; if the number occurs for several years in a row, it marks a period of significant change in your life.

2 The Essence Number 2 marks a time when patience is paramount, especially where new relationships are concerned. Anxiety is likely if it remains in effect for several years.

3 The Essence Number 3 is linked with happiness, and especially with extending your social circles. If you are lucky enough to have the 3 persist for several years, you are likely to remember the time fondly.

4 The Essence Number 4 signifies a period when you will need to work hard to achieve the goals you seek. If the number occurs for several years, you may find it a long struggle; however, the returns should make the effort worthwhile.

5 The Essence Number 5 is one of rapid change—during this time, you may well experience unexpected freedom, especially the chance to travel. Self-discipline will pay off in the long-run.

6 The Essence Number 6 denotes a period of domestic activities and long relationships. This comes with a need to take responsibilities seriously, especially if it extends for several years.

7 The Essence Number 7 is often associated with self-discovery and learning. If the number persists for several years, it is important to avoid becoming too introverted.

8 The Essence Number 8 is often linked with material advancement, especially career development. It is a time when you need to put in a considerable amount of hard work, something that can take a personal toll if it lasts for a protracted period.

9 The Essence Number 9 is usually connected to periods of intense emotional activity. When it persists for several years, you risk becoming drained, so it is important to be aware of this.

left *Determining the Essence Numbers for each year of your life is a straightforward, but somewhat lengthy process, involving the creation of a chart from the letters in your name.*

right *The Essence Numbers can be used to determine how to react to certain issues. The 2, for example, marks a time when patience is paramount, especially where relationships are concerned.*

THE TRANSIT LETTERS

SPECIAL K Each Transit Letter has particular connotations —"K," for instance, is associated with relationships, sensitivity, and spirituality.

In numerology, the letters that make up your full birth name can be used to derive what are known as "The Transits." Each letter has particular connotations and is associated with periods of time that last for between one and nine years. The Transits are identified as part of the process of creating an Essences Chart, and, as with the Essences, should be considered in conjunction with the results of the Personal Year reading. If a Transit letter is repeated, it magnifies that letter's interpretation.

As an illustration of the principle, it can be seen in the Essences chart on page 63 that Jimi Hendrix was twenty years old in 1962, and his corresponding Transit letters for the year are N, L, and D. The meanings of these letters are shown opposite.

Number of Years

1	2	3	4	5	6	7	8	9
A	B	C	D	E	F	G	H	I
J	K	L	M	N	O	P	Q	R
S	T	U	V	W	X	Y	Z	

The number of years each Transit Letter lasts for.

The letters that make up your full birth name can be used to identify "The Transits."

Below *Life is a journey that is full of choices. The way ahead is not always clear, but sometimes you come to a fork in the road and must make a key decision.*

Keywords for the Transit Letters

A Creativity. Change.

B Relationships. Working with others.

C Sociability. Creativity.

D Self-reliance. Hard work.

E Change. Travel. Romance.

F Responsibility. Security. Romance.

G Introspection. Introversion. Study / Learning.

H Security. Ambition. Hard work.

I Emotions. Sensitivity. Anxiety. Creativity.

J Security. Change. Anxiety.

K Relationships. Sensitivity. Spirituality.

L Sociability. Creativity. Hedonism.

M Practicality. Hard work. Security.

N Change. Travel. Romance. Opportunity.

O Responsibility. Security. Learning.

P Introspection. Introversion. Study/Learning.

Q Security. Ambition. Hard work. Opportunity.

R Compassion. Emotions. Sensitivity. Anxiety. Creativity.

S Creativity. Change. Emotional. Ambition.

T Relationships. Sensitivity. Spirituality. Anxiety.

U Sociability. Creativity. Hedonism. Anxiety.

V Practicality. Ambition. Hard work. Security.

W Change. Travel. Adventure. Romance. Opportunity.

X Domesticity. Responsibility. Security. Learning.

Y Introspection. Introversion. Spirituality.

Z Security. Ambition. Dedication. Anxiety.

above *The Transit Letters should be considered in conjunction with the results of the Personal Year reading.*

above *Some Transit Letters, such as "X," signify a love of domesticity, whereas others, such as "B" and "T" are associated with relationships.*

RELATIONSHIP ANALYSIS

Numerology can be used to reveal a number of factors to do with relationships. It can, for instance, identify which character traits are likely to result in harmony, and which are not. This is just as applicable to potential future relationships as to those which are already underway. It is important to realize that if you identify any possible conflicts, they should not be seen as dead-ends, but simply as areas that might need special consideration. For example, if one partner in a relationship likes taking part in sports, but the other does not, this is no reason for them to stop seeing one another. All it means is that both must consider the other's position, and make room for this in their lives. If they are able to achieve this, then harmony will be promoted, and the relationship can flourish.

The actual Relationship Analysis is performed by comparing the attributes highlighted by the respective partner's Destiny Numbers and Life Path Numbers (see pages 21 and 23).

right *Numerology can be used to identify which character traits are likely to result in harmony, and which are not. Possible conflicts should not be seen as dead-ends, but simply as areas that might need special consideration.*

opposite page *If both parties in a relationship are able to consider the other's position and make room for it in their lives, then harmony will be promoted, and the partnership can flourish.*

Create a Relationship Comparison Chart

The method is to complete the chart below with the relevant information:

	Partner 1	Partner 2	Attribute
Life Path Numbers			
Destiny Numbers			

The respective attributes can then be compared and examined for compatibility.

BABY NAMES

Baby Names

opposite page *The Birth Day Number is simply the date on which a child was delivered; it is used in conjunction with the Life Path Number.*
right *When choosing a name, some people may choose to be guided by the numerological aspects in the hope that this will promote both family harmony and the child's long-term prospects.*
below *Choosing a baby's name always raises a number of questions—should it be named after a family member, a favored celebrity, or even a place that has significant meaning to the parents?*

Choosing a name for a baby always raises a number of questions—things such as whether it should be named after a family member, a favored celebrity, or even a place that has significant meaning to the parents. Alternatively, they may select a name simply because they like it. Some people, however, may choose to be guided by the numerological aspects in the hope that this will promote both family harmony and the child's long-term prospects. In this case, the first thing to do is to ensure that the proposed name is compatible with those of the parents. Once this has been established, the next stage is to choose a middle name. A perennial problem is that of who should have final say in the matter. Perhaps you could agree with your partner—or alternatively with a close friend or relative—that you choose the baby's first name and they choose the middle name? This approach can work well and overcome disagreements about which names work best.

and so determining the Core Aspects is not straightforward. One way around this is to work from the expected date, and then calculate everything for a few days either side—this could be a long process though!

The details to check for can include all of the following:

Name compatibility
You can check to see if the proposed names are likely to promote harmony within the family using the methods previously outlined in "Relationship Analysis." The first place to start is with the parents' names, and then those of any siblings. Clearly, it is important to avoid names which are likely to lead to conflict.

The Destiny Number
The Destiny Number is used to assess what opportunities may come along during an individual's lifetime as well as how they may relate to those around them. As this is derived from the birth name rather than the date, choosing a suitable appellation is an important matter.

Find out which baby names might work best for you
The first stage of assessing the numerological issues around naming a baby is to make a list of all the proposed names, and then to examine each of them in turn. It is important to remember that if the baby has not been born, the precise birth date will not be known,

The Life Path Number

The Life Path Number can be used to reveal an individual's inherent attributes and abilities, as well as where their journey through life may take them. As this aspect is determined by the birth date, however, any pre-birth calculations would have to take account of possible variations in the actual day of delivery.

The Birth Day Number

The Birth Day Number is simply the date on which someone was born, and is used in conjunction with the Life Path Number to reveal what they could make of any attributes they were born with. As mentioned above, any pre-birth calculations need to take account of possible variations in the actual day of delivery.

Personal Year Number

The Personal Year Number is used to determine how the coming year is likely to turn out. Finding the actual number is very straightforward—the number of the birth month is added to the birth day. The resultant number is then added to the year number.

The Planes of Expression

The Planes of Expression are identified from the letters used in a name, and reveal much about the way an individual behaves and what their overall life potential may be. Consequently, appropriate name selection is very important.

Soul Urge

The Soul Urge describes the things that make up a person's innermost desires as well as the things they love or hate. It is determined by the vowels that are used in their name, and so are directly influenced by the name that is chosen.

Personality Number

The Personality Number, which identifies many character traits, is dictated by the numerical values of the consonants of each of the full birth names.

Blending the Core Aspects

The Core Aspects can only be properly analyzed by compiling a Blending Chart. As this is a somewhat lengthy process that relies to a large extent on matters determined by the actual delivery date, it is probably best left until after the child has been born. The Blending Chart can then be used to reveal how the Core Aspects are likely to interact with each other during the child's life.

Harmonious and Discordant Aspects

As with the Core Aspects, identifying the Harmonious and Discordant Aspects is probably best left until after the child has been born. Once the birth date of the child is known, it is possible to reveal which of the child's Core Aspects are going to conflict with each other, and which will be beneficial. Then to a certain extent you can be forearmed for the future.

THE PLANES OF EXPRESSION
The Planes of Expression are identified from the letters used in a person's name, and reveal much about the way they behave and what their overall life potential may be.

NAME CHANGING

below *Although many aspects of numerology are locked in by your full birth name, there is little doubt that changing your name will have a consequent effect on your journey through life. Most people alter their names at one time or another—this may be due to the acquisition of a nickname, through marriage, or in more extreme cases, via a legal name change.*

Although many aspects of numerology are fixed by the full birth name, there is little doubt that changing your name will have a consequent effect on your journey through life. At one time or another, most people alter their names in some way. It may be that they acquire a nickname, get married, or in some cases, go through the full legal process to change their formal name. Other things can change, also—in the transition from being a child to an adult, a person may find that instead of being addressed by their first name, they are called Mr, Mrs, or Ms. Likewise, the attainment of social rank may result in a title change. On successful completion of a PhD, for instance, this may change to "Dr," or on joining the armed forces,

it could be replaced with a military rank. Each time that a name is changed, it will have an impact on the way that other people respond to it. There is no question that name changes that result from honors being bestowed, such as the addition of "Sir" or "Lord" will change how a person is perceived. Many famous people in the entertainment industry rely on alternative names for one reason or another. We have already looked at John Wayne's numerology, and the fact that his real name was Marion Michael Morrison. Would he have ever got to play the part of the tough guy if he had stuck with the name Marion? This is, of course, something that we will never know— but we can make our suppositions.

Name changing is an emotive business that is bound to have an impact on your journey through life.

CHANGING NAMES
If you are unhappy with your name, you need not feel tied to it—it is easy to get it changed legally.

SCALE THE HEIGHTS
Many people change their names in order to get ahead in their chosen career—especially those in the music and movie industries, where it can make a significant difference.

The last word

In this book we have attempted to present the mysterious subject of numerology in an informed and entertaining manner. It is vital, however, that anyone who wishes to learn from it understands the main principle that underlies the study. That is, the numbers cannot do anything on their own. Just because they indicate that you have the capacity to be good at something does not mean that you will be good at it. If you wish to achieve your

above *There is no question that the name changes which result from honors being bestowed will influence how a person is perceived.*

potential, YOU have to put the work in. If there is one thing the author would like you to take from this book it is this: everyone is capable of much more than they would ever believe of themselves. If you want to make the most of yourself:

JUST GET OUT THERE AND DO IT!

READING CHARTS & WORKSHEETS

Letter to Number Conversion Chart:

1	2	3	4	5	6	7	8	9
A	B	C	D	E	F	G	H	I
J	K	L	M	N	O	P	Q	R
S	T	U	V	W	X	Y	Z	

The Destiny Number

Your Destiny Number is found by taking your full birth name and converting it into numeric form:

Fill these boxes in with your written name:

First Name:..

....

Middle Name:..

....

Last Name:...

....

Fill these boxes in with the number equivalents of each name, reduced to a single digit:

First Name:..

....

Middle Name:..

....

Last Name:...

....

Add the above numbers together, and reduce them to a single digit:

Destiny Number:.....................................

NUMBER 6 The number 6 Destiny suggests that the direction of growth in your lifetime will be toward a greater sense of responsibility, love, and balance.

The Life Path Number

Your Life Path Number is found by summing together the numbers that make up your birth date:

Fill these boxes in with your birth details:

Birth Day:..

....

Birth Month:..

....

Birth Year:...

....

Add the above numbers together, and reduce them to a single digit:

Life Path Number:..................................

The Personal Year Number

Your Personal Year Number is found from your birth day, birth month, and birth year:

Fill these boxes in with your birth details:

Birth Day:..

....

Birth Month:..

....

Birth Year:...

....

Add your Birth Day Number to your Birth Month Number, and reduce them to a single digit:

a) Reduced sum of Birth Day +
    Birth Month =.......................................

Next reduce your Birth Year to a single digit.

For e.g.: 2009 = 2 + 0 + 0 + 9 = 11; 1+ 1 = 2
b) Reduced Birth Year =.............................

Now add a) and b) together to find your Personal Year Number:

Personal Year Number:.................................

The Soul Urge Number

Your Soul Urge is found by converting the vowels in your full birth name into numeric values.

List the vowels in each part of your full birth name:

First Name:.................................
....

Middle Name:.................................
....

Last Name:.................................
....

Convert the vowels into numerics, add values for each name together, and reduce to a single digit:

First Name:.................................
....

Middle Name:.................................
....

Last Name:.................................
....

Soul Urge Number: ....

The Birth Day Number

The Birth Day Number is the date on which you were born; it is not reduced to a single digit.

Birth Day Number:.................................

The Personality Number

Your Personality Number is found from the numeric values of the consonants in your name.

List the consonants in each part of your full birth name:

First Name:.................................
....

Middle Name:.................................
....

Last Name:.................................
....

Convert the consonants into numerics, add each name together, and reduce to a single digit:

First Name:.................................
....

Middle Name:.................................
....

Last Name:.................................
....

Finally, add all three together and reduce to a single digit (unless it is a Master Number):

Personality Number:.................................

NUMBER 2 Those with a 2 Destiny Number have a natural inclination toward understanding people.

NUMBER 28 People with a Birth Day Number of 28 are considered to be independent and self-confident, although they can also become repressed or dominating.

Finally, add all three together and reduce to a single digit:

Your Destiny Number is found by taking your full birth name and converting it into numeric form using a special formula.

The Growth Number

Your Growth Number is found by converting the letters in your first name into their numeric equivalents, and then adding them together:

List the letters in your first name here:

First Name:..

....

Convert the letters to their number equivalents:

First Name:..

....

Add the numbers together and reduce them to a single digit:

Growth Number:..

....

above *If you apply the principles of numerology that are outlined in this book, you might find that you discover a new well of peace, contentment, and generally greater happiness in your life.*

The Habit Challenge Number

Your Habit Challenge Number is found by adding up the number of letters in your full birth name:

Fill these boxes in with your written name:

First Name:..

....

Middle Name:..

....

Last Name:..

....

Write down the number of letters used to make up each part of your name (i.e. "John" = 4)

First Name:..

....

Middle Name:..

....

Last Name:..

....

Finally, add all three together and reduce to a single digit (unless it is a Master Number):

Habit Challenge Number:..

The Maturity Number

Your Maturity Number is found by adding your Destiny Number and your Life Path Number:

Write your Destiny Number here:....................

Write your Life Path Number here:....................

Add your Destiny and your Life Path Number—if necessary, reduce them to a single digit:

Maturity Number:..

NOTES

use this page to work out your calculations

ONLINE RESOURCES

General numerology websites:

www.numerology.org.uk
The official website of the Association
Internationale de Numerologues
Incorporating the
Connaissance School of Numerology

www.numbersru.com
Chaldean Numerology Charts and Readings
since 1984

www.numerology4you.com
Find out the Secret Knowledge that
Numerology can tell you about yourself and
others.
by Keith Abbott

www.astrology-numerology.com
Astrology and Numerology presented by
Michael McClain

http://thedreamtime.com/spirit/numerology.
html

http://en.wikipedia.org/wiki/Numerology

www.numberquest.com

Introductions to numerology:

www.numerology-free.com

www.crystalinks.com/numerology.html

www.themystica.com/mystica/articles/n/
numerology.html

www.numerologyinfo.org

Free online numerology reports:

http://affinity-numerology.com/cgi-bin/
numerology.cgi

http://cafeastrology.com/numerology2

www.paulsadowski.com/Numbers.asp

www.facade.com/numerology

Religious numerology links:

www.carm.org/questions/numbers.htm

www.sephar.net/index.htm

www.bibletexts.com/glossary/number-
symbolism.htm

Advanced numerology links:

www.psyche.com/psyche/qbl/comparative_
numerology.html

above *There is a wealth of information about numerology on the internet, all available at the click of a computer's mouse.*

BIBLIOGRAPHY

Adrienne, Carol; *The Complete Numerology Kit*. Plume, 1987.

Campbell, Florence; *Your Days Are Numbered.* The Gateway, 1931.

Cheiro; *Cheiro's Book of Numbers*. Arco Publishing, Inc. 1964.

Cooper, D. Jason; *Understanding Numerology*. Aquarian Press, 1986.

Davis, John J.; *Biblical Numerology: A Basic Study of the Use of Numbers in the Bible*. Baker Book House, 1981.

Decoz, Hans; *Numerology*. Penguin Group. 2001.

DiPietro, Sylvia; *Live Your Life By The Numbers*. Penguin Books, 1991.

Drayer, Ruth; *Numerology: The Power in Numbers*. Square One Publications, 2003.

Goodwin, Matthew Oliver; *Numerology: The Complete Guide, Volume 1, The Personality Reading*. Newcastle Publishing Company, 1981.

Goodwin, Matthew Oliver; *Numerology: The Complete Guide, Volume 2, Advanced Personality Analysis and Reading the Past, Present, and Future*. Newcastle Publishing Company, 2000.

Hitchcock, Helyn; *Helping Yourself With Numerology*. Parker Publishing Company Inc., 1972.

Javane F & Bunker; D; *Numerology and the Divine Triangle*. Para Research, Mar 1979

Juno, Jordan; *The Romance In Your Name*. Rowny Press, 1965.

Keller, Joyce & Jack; *The Complete Book of Numerology*. St. Martin's, 2001.

Konraad, Sandor; *Numerology: Key to the Tarot*. Schiffer Pub., 1983.

Lawrence; Shirley Blackwell, *Behind Numerology*. Newcastle Publishing Co., Ltd., 1989.

Line, Julia; *Discover Numerology*. Sterling Publishing Company, Inc., 1993.

Line, Julia; *The Numerology Workbook*. Sterling Publishing Company, Inc., 1990.

Lingerman, Hal A.; *Living Your Destiny*. Samuel Weiser, Inc., 1992.

McCants, Glynis; *Glynis Has Your Number: Discover What Life Has in Store for You Through the Power of Numerology!* Hyperion. 2005.

Ravindra, Kumar; *Secrets of Numerology*. Anmol Publications, 2004

Strayhorn, Lloyd; *Numbers And You*. Ballantine Books, 1990.

Taylor, Ariel Yvon; *Numerology Made Plain*. Newcastle Publishing Company Inc., 1973.

Vaughan, Richard Blackmore; *Numbers As Symbols Of Self-Discovery*. Phantasy Press. 1973.

Vega, Phyllis; *Numerology for Baby Names: Use the Ancient Art of Numerology to Give Your Baby a Head Start in Life*. Dell Pub., 1998.

Webster, Richard; *Chinese Numerology*, 2005.

INDEX

PICTURE CREDITS

The majority of the photographs in this book were taken or supplied especially for it by the author and the packager, Focus Publishing. The images on the following pages are copyright Image Source/Getty Images: 29 (bottom left); 47; 55 (top); 64; 65; 70 (bottom left); 76.

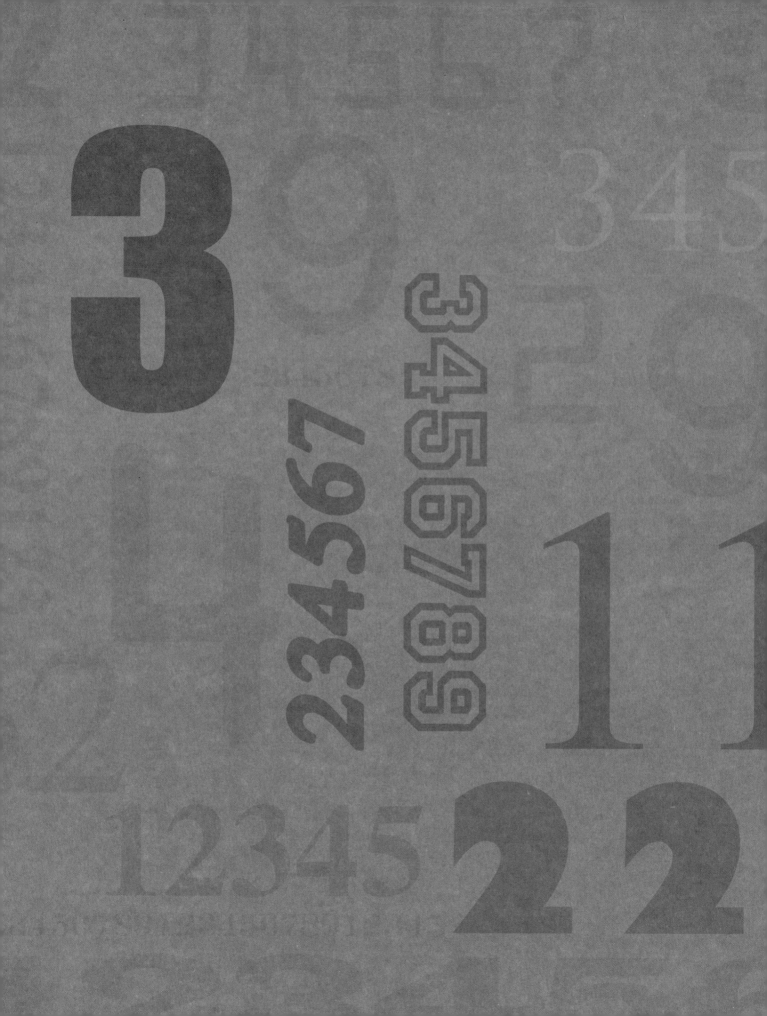